BLOOM
IN YOUR
WINTER
SEASON

DEBORAH MALONE

with Twenty-Three Contributing Authors

Deborah
Malone
Ps 92:14-15

LAMP POST

publishers

BLOOM
IN YOUR
WINTER
SEASON

DEBORAH MALONE

WITH:

Marla Aycock • Michelle Bengtson • Debra Lynn Collins

Valerie Dennis • Patricia Durgin • Terri Gillespie

Sherye S. Green • Patty Smith Hall • Linda Kozar

Marlys Johnson Lawry • Delores Liesner • Kathi Macias

Beverly Nault • Lisa Nelson • Vernet Clemons Nettles

Gail Pallotta • Cindy Pope • Rita Prochazka

Lorilyn Roberts • Stephanie Rodda • Cynthia Simmons

Janice Thompson • Christine Trimpe

BLOOM IN YOUR WINTER SEASON
by Deborah Malone

Scripture quotations taken from the Amplified® Bible (AMP), Copyright © 2015 by The Lockman Foundation. Used by permission. lockman.org

Scripture quotations marked (ESV) are taken from THE HOLY BIBLE, ENGLISH STANDARD VERSION®, Copyright © 2001 by Crossway, a publishing ministry of Good News Publishers. Used by permission.

Scripture quotations marked (NLT) taken from the Holy Bible, New Living Translation, copyright ©1996, 2004, 2007, 2013, 2015 by Tyndale House Foundation. Used by permission of Tyndale House Publishers, Inc., Carol Stream, Illinois 60188. All rights reserved.

Scripture quotations marked (NASB) are taken from the NEW AMERICAN STANDARD BIBLE®, Copyright © 1960, 1962, 1963, 1968, 1971, 1972, 1973, 1975, 1977, 1995 by The Lockman Foundation. Used by permission.

Scripture quotations marked (NIV) are taken from THE HOLY BIBLE, NEW INTERNATIONAL VERSION®. Copyright © 1973, 1978, 1984, 2011 by Biblica, Inc.™. Used by permission of Zondervan.

Scripture quotations marked (NKJV) are taken from the NEW KING JAMES VERSION®. Copyright © 1982 by Thomas Nelson, Inc. Used by permission. All rights reserved.

Scripture quotations marked (TLV) taken from the Holy Scriptures, Tree of Life Version. Copyright © 2014, 2016 by the Tree of Life Bible Society. Used by permission of the Tree of Life Bible Society.

Published by:

LAMP POST publishers
SPRING VALLEY · CALIFORNIA
www.lamppostpublishers.com

Trade Paperback: ISBN-13 # 979-8-8692-5529-7

Contents

Introduction

Welcome to the Winter Warriors club. A club made up of "seasoned" women who have a desire to give their heart to Abba, even during the phases of their winter season. Maybe you've been going through changes that have you discouraged and ready to throw in the towel.

Change is inevitable: hearing aids, eyeglasses, and a knee replacement are just a few things I've already experienced. Not to mention the changes to my body shape and size—yikes! Maybe you've been through some of these changes, too. If we dwell too long on the inevitable, it can be easy to get discouraged and want to just sit down and give up.

But if you're reading this, then you are looking for ways to keep on keeping on, even during these changes. And I hope this Bible Study, which features several "seasoned" women from the Bible, will encourage you to keep on serving our Abba until your last breath.

In this study you will be treated to twenty-four devotions by "seasoned" authors who continue to be active for the Lord in many ways—large or small—it is all for God's glory.

You will hear me saying often, "God did not stamp an expiration date on our forehead." While studying these women from the Bible, you will discover that God can and will use you even in your winter season.

As my friend Beth says, "There's only one alternative to growing old." And we all know what that is—something we will all have to face eventually, but until then, let's make a pact to grow old as "seasoned" women being Winter Warriors for our Abba!

Deborah Malone

BLOOM
IN YOUR
WINTER
SEASON

Chapter One

ANNA & MIRIAM

Whose Ministry Is This Anyway?

BEVERLY NAULT

Whatever you do, work heartily,
as for the Lord and not for men.
COLOSSIANS 3:23 ESV

Two prophetesses were used by God. Miriam and Anna. Miriam provides a perplexing tale of obedience that turns into a cautionary tale. As a widow, Anna lived most of her adult life as a widow but was rewarded with the best Christmas gift ever in her golden years. Which one am I modeling to my family, church, and especially the younger women who watch me? God used Miriam to ensure that her baby brother Moses was spared in that famous story that still gives me pause. And she was instrumental in helping lead her people out of slavery in Egypt. What a gal, right?

Anna buried her husband at an early age and then dedicated her life to serving the Lord. She even moved onto the temple grounds to be near the holiest of holies.

These servants are both inspirations but also a contrast in serving Him. While Anna waited on the Lord in humility and quiet grace, Miriam became a complainer expecting power and accolades in jealousy of her brother Moses.

Many years ago, I helped launch a ministry that bloomed and flourished until it was one of our small town's most successful and well-attended women's ministries. The activities thrived, and our numbers grew. Then suddenly, my husband's job changed, and we announced our departure.

I prepared for the next meeting of "my" ministry and the expected appreciation. I prepared a speech and carefully selected the perfect outfit for my moment in the spotlight. I even practiced in the mirror how to be humble at their gushing gratitude.

On the morning of my last meeting, I sat waiting expectantly for the leader, Sue, to call on me, to thank me for my service, and ask me to come up and say a few words. I checked my hair and lipstick.

But her invitation never came during the announcements. The speaker took the stage. I fought back tears as she spoke. Then a thought occurred. They have planned something so big to honor me they scheduled it after the regular meeting so we could take our time reminiscing! I looked around at the faces of "my" staff, wondering how they could hide their anticipation from me. Indeed, they were doing a great job!

Then the speaker finished. The benediction delivered. The meal plates cleared away.

I made it to my car without breaking down, but once there, I bawled.

"Why didn't they thank me, God? How could Sue have ignored the hours I spent to make this ministry the success it is today?"

I spent the next few busy days packing and fuming. On our final day in town, the phone rang as we were cleaning the house and loading our suitcases to drive to our new state and new home.

My husband answered. "It's Sue."

"I don't want to talk to her. Tell her I have a headache."

He held the phone out to me, not taking no for an answer.

"Fine." I took a deep breath and blurted. "Hello, Sue, I'm really busy we have to get on the road and—"

"Bev. I just opened the note you sent telling us you were moving. It was stuck to another envelope. I'm so sorry I didn't read it in time, or we would have announced your departure at the meeting and given you a proper farewell. Can I at least come over and give you a hug before you go?"

God was teaching me a lesson. This was never MY ministry, it was His, and I had been honored to serve in a leadership position. I had done my work well. But I hadn't done it entirely for Him.

Like Miriam, I was expecting accolades for my work. While I didn't do something as miraculous and world changing as saving baby Moses, the ministry was changing the world for the women who attended. In the final hour, literally, He showed me my place through that phone call from Sue.

When Miriam obeyed her mother to place Moses in the reeds, she was doing the Lord's work. But later, when she complained that He didn't seem to favor her as He did Moses, she made it about her, as I had done. Eventually, she was afflicted with leprosy and died before reaching the Promised Land.

Anna served without complaint, and as a young widow, I can imagine she had plenty to complain about. However, in her final hours, she was rewarded with a glimpse of the baby Jesus, who had come into the world as our Savior.

I know I will see Jesus in heaven or on earth if that day comes before I graduate. And when I do, I will thank Him for reminding me that it is His creation, and I serve at His pleasure and for His glory, not mine.

Application Question:

Have you ever caught yourself complaining about not getting enough praise for the work you'd done in service to the Lord?

Prayer:

Lord, remind me that my service is for you and when I diminish myself you receive glory and honor.

Lord, thank You for allowing me to serve You continually for Your kingdom. I am here to serve in whatever large or small capacity you desire, without complaint, until the day I kneel at your feet in humble adoration. Amen

Beverly Nault is the author of the beloved Seasons of Cherryvale series, "where neighbors care, gardeners share, and God allows do-overs." She writes Fresh Start Stories because everyone needs one from time to time. You can connect with Beverly at www.beverlynault.com.

God's Timing Is Perfect

CYNTHIA SIMMONS

For a thousand years in your sight are but as yesterday
when it is past, or as a watch in the night.
PSALM 90:4 ESV

I like to get things done, and when I pray, I expect answers immediately. After all, I can place an order and receive that item the next day. I grab packaged food from my refrigerator, pop it in the microwave, and serve dinner within a few minutes. Why can't God follow that same pattern? My needs are urgent. Surely, he knows that. If only I had a magic formula to induce him to hurry.

God works on his own timetable. (Psalm 90:4 ESV) Let's consider how the Lord designed natural processes. I enjoy baking bread and filling the house with that luscious aroma. However, I know I must soften the yeast in water for ten minutes before combining it with the flour, eggs, and oil. The dough must rise twice so the yeast will grow and release gases. If I shorten the process, I will damage the texture of the bread.

God's timing is perfect. He planned the coming of Christ from the foundation of the world. Imagine how long Israel waited for the promised Messiah. In Genesis, God told Adam and Eve the seed of the woman would destroy Satan. Years later, he promised

Abraham his offspring would bless the entire world. Years passed before God promised King David his son would rule on the throne forever. In Daniel chapter nine, angels revealed the timing of the anointed one based on a decree given to rebuild Jerusalem. So, the Jewish people had a rough idea of when the Messiah would come. But after the last prophet in the Old Testament, the Israelites did not hear from God for four hundred years. Many people lived and died from the moment God foretold what he would do and the actual event. But people who trusted in the Lord knew he would keep his promise. The prophetess Anna was one of those people. God honored her by including her, her father Phanuel, and their entire tribe of Asher in the Bible. How amazing!

Once her husband passed away, Anna worshiped the Lord, fasted, and prayed daily, waiting for God to fulfill his promise. Think about praying every day for eighty-four years. Would you get weary praying for that long with no answers? Imagine Anna's joy when Mary, Joseph, and Jesus entered the temple to fulfill the decreed Old Testament rites. Anna was so close to the Lord that she knew that after all those years and all those prayers, she stood in the presence of the Messiah. Here was the person God promised to Adam and Eve, Abraham, David, and Daniel. Thrilled, she snatched everyone who came by to share the wonderful news.

Anna's story touched me deeply. As an older woman, I long to follow her example. That means I stop focusing on my immediate situation. Events going on around me may seem crucial. But are they really? Will this situation even matter in a hundred years? Probably not. Instead, I will bring my need to him and focus on God's eternal plan because he has a way of working things out. Each day I will set aside time to pray while realizing I must wait for God. My heavenly father has his hand on the timing. I can rest and pray with confidence.

Application Questions:

What are you praying for that God doesn't seem to be in a hurry to answer as quickly as you'd like? How can you rest assured that His timing is perfect?

Prayer:

Father, when I grow weary of waiting, remind me that your timing is not always our timing. Help me to remember that your timing is perfect. Amen

Cynthia L Simmons and her husband have five grown children. She loves hot tea, orchids, and historical research. Her ragdoll cats often sit by her when she writes. Cynthia has written historical fiction, mysteries, Bible studies, homeschool curriculum, and hosts *Heart of the Matter Radio* podcast. You can connect with Cynthia at www.clsimmons.com.

Age or Experience.
Do they affect our spiritual impact?

MARLA AYCOCK

There was a prophetess, Anna, the daughter of Phanuel,
of the tribe of Asher. She was very old and had lived
with her husband for seven years after her marriage
and then as a widow at eighty-four. She did not leave
the area of the temple but was serving and worshiping
night and day with fasting and prayers.
LUKE 2:36-38 AMPLIFIED BIBLE

Golden hair and bright blue eyes accentuated the little girl's face as she sat content in a sandbox building make-believe castles. She didn't see the impending danger as her big brother snuck up behind her with evil intent. His fists full of sand were soon pressed into her open eyes.

Her piercing screams sliced the air.

The blinding dirt and painful grit brought ear-splitting cries for help. Her anguish intensified as her mother scolded her for the loud, shrill response. Born with a compassionate nature, when her brother received an old-fashioned spanking for his prank, she stood outside the door and cried over his pain.

As I recall this memory, I see how Jesus' mercy was already developing in my young heart. I realize this is exactly what Jesus does when we mess up. He takes no delight in the consequences of our bad decisions, but he also came into a world filled with people whose eyes were filled with sand, and He wept.

In Luke's gospel, full of what the Holy Spirit had revealed to him, Simeon would live to witness the Messiah before he died. The Spirit prompted him to go to the temple just as Mary and Joseph entered for the ceremony of Mary's purification and Jesus' dedication to the Lord. Simeon took the baby in his arms and proclaimed, "*Now, Lord, you are releasing Your bondservant to leave this world in peace. My eyes have seen Your Salvation...A light for revelation to the Gentiles and to bring praise, honor, and glory to your people Israel*" (Luke 2:29-32 Amplified Bible).

At that very moment, Anna, the prophetess, enters. Let's examine her life. She'd experienced the pain of sand in her own eyes. Widowed after only seven years of marriage, childless and likely with meager provisions to live on. Whether you're four or eighty-four, God desires to exhibit His wisdom and compassion through you to the next generation. You're never too old, too young, or too broken. Notice how aware Anna is of the events on God's timeline in her world.

Anna, too, came up at that very moment and verified the babe was indeed the awaited Messiah and... "*began praising and giving thanks to God, and continued to speak of Him to all who were looking for redemption and the deliverance of Jerusalem*" (Luke 2:38 Amplified Bible).

Maybe the removal of Anna's husband, the lack of a child, plus the difficult life of a widow gradually removed the sand from her eyes. Perhaps her heart became tenderized through suffering as worldly distractions were removed.

"Sometimes God allows what he hates; to accomplish what he loves" (Joni Erickson Tada).

Anna was old but never stopped praying, prophesying, and looking for the Messiah. If you think you must be young to impact your generation, notice the contrast between Mary, the teenage mother of Jesus the Messiah, and the elderly Anna. Both Anna and Mary were strong in God's grace and highly favored. They both longed for and recognized God's Son amid the messiness of their lives and world.

Are you feeling too old, too tired, and worn as you wait for Jesus' return? Two-thousand years makes Anna's wait seem short, but it's no less sure. Look around you! Like Anna saw her world aligning with the first coming of Christ, become aware of how your world is positioning itself with Christ's second return. Speak to all who will listen. The fields are ripe unto harvest. Our ministries are never limited by our age. In fact, our golden years are a blessing and enlarged both our wisdom and borders of ministry.

Just like Anna recognized the first coming of Christ, there couldn't be any higher purpose for older women to fulfill than to recognize the Biblical signs everywhere of the coming rapture and Christ's second return.

Application Question:

Who are the people in your life, Christian or not, with whom you can begin to drop seeds of hope, peace, and truth about the love of Jesus and destroy the frightening things the enemy wants to paralyze them with?

Two Suggestions:

Check out and share the docudrama Before the Wrath *and the new crowd-funded series* The Chosen, *that's having a significant impact on the gospel of Jesus through-out the world.*

Prayer:

Dear Heavenly Father,

    Broaden the boundaries of my spiritual vision that is rich with age and experience to speak truth with grace fearlessly to those in my sphere of influence. When the fruits of your Spirit reign, these qualities: love, joy, peace, patience, kindness, goodness, faithfulness, gentleness, and self-control, will spill out of me. As I receive and walk in these precious gifts you bought for me through the cruelest death possible, may I ever be mindful to pay them forward to all I encounter today. Amen.

Marla Aycock spent most of her life in music education and ministry while raising a complex trio of daughters. Her dramatic memoir, *Grief is Not My Future*, is based on the experiences surrounding her young-est daughter, Esther. She has been a member of Calhoun Area Writers, Georgia Writers Association, and the Christian Authors Guild. Marla and her husband live in the foothills of the beautiful North Georgia mountains. One of Marla's greatest joys is to hear from you. You can connect with Marla at www.marlagayle@yahoo.com.

Must We Decrease?

TERRI GILLESPIE

[Jesus] must increase, while I must decrease.
JOHN 3:30 TLV

How would you like to be Moses' older sister, Miriam?

Scholars and various commentaries credit Miriam as a protector, worshiper, and prophetess—yet all that pales in comparison to her little brother Moses. Miriam's resume is impressive, especially for the 13th century BCE. That is, until Moses returns to Egypt with signs and wonders. Once the LORD frees the Jewish people from over 300 years of slavery,[1] Moses designates Aaron as High Priest of the Tabernacle. And Miriam, she gets to play the tambourine. Well, she does a bit more than that.

When she attempts to assert her role as big sister and corrects her younger brother, Moses, about his wife, that didn't go over well (Numbers 12:10). She ended up with leprosy. Thankfully, Moses pleaded with the LORD for her to be healed.

I've always wondered, after that incident and decades in the wilderness, when someone spoke about Miriam, did the younger people say, "Miriam who?"

---

1 Prior to that they had favor in Egypt because of Joseph.

"You know, Moses' and Aaron's older sister."

"Moses had a sister?"

Miriam's journey from "first"—first child, first one to protect her brother, first prophetess, first to teach the Children of Israel how to worship, and one of the guides to lead the mass of people out of Egypt—to near obscurity had to be a difficult one. Yes, Miriam made some mistakes, but if we take the whole of her life in Scriptures, she should be remembered for her bravery, too.

Remember John the Immerser? Wooly, loud, sometimes offensive, but a powerful prophet who made the way for his cousin, our Messiah. I love what John said when his disciples wanted him to make himself more visible and admired like his cousin.

Will there be a day when we must decrease so the younger generation can increase? If it hasn't happened yet, yes, it will. Actually, it *should* be that way—others stepped aside for us. But does that mean our work and purpose are no longer significant? Absolutely not!

Recently, my husband and I had to close a ministry into which we had invested our blood, sweat, and sobs. It was difficult to not feel like failures or that we could ever be relevant to ministry again. Since 1973, we have followed Jesus and seen amazing miracles and been part of historical events that some people only read about in books. But to those who see hubby and me sitting in a pew, all they see are two old people.

Here's the thing: When our Heavenly Father called us to work for His purposes, He called us *before* we were knit in our mother's womb. Won't that purpose change as we are seasoned with years and experiences? Did our ministry just spring from nothing or was it gradual so that He and others could train us? Why *wouldn't* our ministry change—we do.

The key is to continually seek His fresh anointing each day. Whatever that is, wherever it takes us, and whomever we touch for His glory.

Fresh. Each. Day. Not striving to keep what we *had* but seek what the LORD has for us *now*.

Without this ministry on our shoulders, we have freedom to answer GOD's calls. Can we trust the LORD to guide us? Because when we do, He will use us no matter our age or abilities.

Application Questions:

Change is often difficult, especially when it feels like our worth is decreasing. Are you struggling with change right now? How are you working through that change? Do you feel like a failure because you aren't "needed" in the same way? What are ways you can seek how you can help in other ways?

Prayer:

Abba, help me to be sensitive to Your Spirit's guidance and not be intimidated with change. Help me learn from Miriam to be there for others but not assert my agenda. In Jesus' Name. Amen.

Terri Gillespie is an award-winning author and speaker. Her women's devotional *Making Eye Contact with GOD* is in its fifteenth year. Her inspirational novels are stories of hope and redemption. You can connect with Terri at www.authorterrigillespie.com.

Anna & Miriam

What do Anna and Miriam have in common? Did you know both were prophetesses appointed by God? Let's start with Miriam first since she is found in the Old Testament.

Read Exodus 15: 20-21

> *Then Miriam the prophet, Aaron's sister, took a tambourine and led all the women as they played their tambourines and danced. And Miriam sang this song. 'Sing to the Lord, for he has triumphed gloriously; he has hurled both horse and rider into the sea.*
>
> *Exodus 15:20-21 NLT*

What description of Miriam appears first in these two verses?

_____
_____
_____
_____

I don't remember, as a child, being taught about Miriam and the great role God gave her during the Exodus.

Were you taught as a child that Miriam was a prophetess? What do you remember being taught about Miriam?

_____

_____

_____

_____

_____

_____

_____

And what is a prophetess anyway? Let's take a little break right here and look up the word prophetess. I'll meet you back here in a minute after conducting my own research.

Okay, I'm back. This is a smidgeon of what I gathered from my research.

> A prophetess is a female prophet. The word prophet comes from the Greek word prophets, which means "spokesman." A prophet in the Bible is a person who proclaims God's Word and therefore speaks for God. A prophetess was, therefore, a spokeswoman for God. The faithful prophet or prophetess was one who, regardless of whether he or she was listened to, spoke everything God said to speak. (www.gotquestions.com)

According to the book, *Women in the Bible for Dummies,* in biblical times, "prophet" or "prophetess" had a different context than it does today. Instead of meaning someone who predicts the future, as it is commonly known today, a prophet in biblical times meant one who was a messenger of God and spoke in his name.

What was your definition of a prophetess?

_____

_____

_____

_____

_____

_____

How does your description compare with what I discovered?

_____

_____

_____

_____

_____

_____

_____

_____

_____

Did you know there were several women in the Bible who were given the title of prophetess? Let's look at some.

Copy the verse Exodus 15:20 below and circle the prophetess in this passage.

_____

_____

_____

_____

_____

_____

Write the following verses and circle the names of the prophetesses in each passage:

Judges 4:4

_____
_____
_____
_____

2 Kings 22:14

_____
_____
_____
_____

Isaiah 8:3 (NIV)

_____
_____
_____
_____

Luke 2:36

_____
_____
_____
_____

Acts 21:8-9

_____
_____
_____
_____

We see there are six instances in the Bible that mention women prophetesses. As we travel the road toward our winter season together, we will learn that God cherished women and often used them to further his message. No matter how old (or young) they were.

Speaking of age, let's do a little detecting and see if we can figure out how old Miriam and Anna were. Let's start with Miriam. We are told in the Bible that Miriam was the older sister of Moses.

Read Exodus 2:1-4. How was Miriam related to Moses?

About this time, a man and woman from the tribe of Levi got married. The woman became pregnant and gave birth to a son. She saw that he was a special baby and kept him hidden for three months. But when she could no longer hide him, she got a basket made of papyrus reeds and waterproofed it with tar and pitch. She put the baby in the basket and laid it among the reeds along the bank of the Nile River. The baby's sister then stood at a distance, watching to see what would happen to him.

Exodus 2:1-4 NLT

_____

_____

_____

_____

_____

_____

Now we know that Miriam was older than Moses. Let's do some more digging and see if we can discover how old Moses was at the time of the Exodus. Do you have a guess?

Read Exodus 7:7. How old were Moses and Aaron when they talked with Pharaoh?

Moses was eighty years old, and Aaron was eighty-three when they made their demands to Pharaoh.

Exodus 7:7 NLT

_____

_____

_____

_____

_____

_____

Aha! The game's afoot, as Sherlock would say. We know Moses was eighty at the time he approached Pharaoh. And we've already discovered Miriam was his older sister. So, if Miriam was five or six years old when she watched out for Moses, that would make her eighty-six during the time of the plagues. And she could have very well been older than six.

I find it amazing that God did not go out and find a strapping young man to lead his chosen people out of Egypt. No, he chose someone who had some age on him, probably because along with age comes wisdom. Isn't it eye-opening to stop and think about how old Moses really was—eighty! That is nothing to sneeze at. Moses had already lived a life full of turmoil and trials. Yet, that is who God chose to lead his people!

Read Deuteronomy 34:7. How old was Moses when he died?

Moses was 120 years old when he died, yet his eyesight was clear, and he was as strong as ever.

Deuteronomy 34:7 NLT

———————————————————————————

———————————————————————————

———————————————————————————

———————————————————————————

Well, that's more than I can say for myself, and I still have a way to go to reach 120. Now that we have these clues, I believe we can estimate how old Miriam was when she was appointed a prophetess and leader of the women during the Exodus.

With the information from above, approximately how old was Miriam when she was a great leader of the women during the Exodus?

———————————————————————————

———————————————————————————

———————————————————————————

———————————————————————————

Are you getting the picture now? We know Moses was already in his eighties, and that puts Miriam in her late eighties or early nineties. And let's not forget that Aaron was in his eighties, also. Wow—can you drink in the fact that God used these brothers and sister in their winter season in such a mighty way? We are only in Chapter One and have already discovered our worth in God's eyes.

But it doesn't stop there. We have many more women to study that God chose to use in their winter season. And we are going to discover that God can and will use us in every season. Remember, Miriam was only a child when she was put in charge of watching after her baby brother, Moses.

A woman's spiritual impact doesn't depend on age or experience. God did not stamp an expiration date on our foreheads! Anna, from the New Testament account in Luke is a perfect example. Get ready to ride a little further on our journey to discovering our worth in God's eyes. Yes! Even in our winter season!

Anna was a prophetess like Miriam. As we have already discovered she is the only named prophetess in the New Testament. There are just a few verses written about Anna, but they are jam packed with nuggets of encouragement. Let's look at those verses.

Read Luke 2:36-38

> *Anna, a prophet, was also there in the Temple. She was the daughter of Phanuel from the tribe of Asher, and she was very old. Her husband died when they had been married only seven years. Then she lived as a widow to the age of eighty-four.[2] She never left the Temple but stayed there day and night, worshiping God with fasting and prayer. She came along just as Simeon was talking with Mary and Joseph, and she began praising God. She talked about the child to everyone who had been waiting expectantly for God to rescue Jerusalem.*
>
> *Luke 2:36-38 NLT*

Let's put our gear in reverse for a minute and discover why Mary and Joseph were in the temple at that time.

Read Luke 2:22-24 to see why Mary and Joseph had brought baby Jesus to the temple.

---

2   Or *She had been a widow for eighty-four years.*

Then it was time for their purification offering, as required by the law of Moses after the birth of a child; so his parents took him to Jerusalem to present him to the Lord. The law of the Lord says, "If a woman's first child is a boy he must be dedicated to the Lord." So they offered the sacrifice required in the law of the Lord—"either a pair of turtle-doves or two young pigeons."

Luke 2:22-24 NLT

_____

_____

_____

_____

Read Leviticus 12:6-7 to find out what the Old Testament has to say about the purification ceremony. Does this help explain the reason Mary and Joseph were at the temple?

When the time of purification is completed for either a son or a daughter, the woman must bring a one-year-old lamb for a burnt offering and a young pigeon or turtledove for a purification offering. She must bring her offerings to the priest at the entrance of the Tabernacle. The priest will then present them to the Lord to purify her. Then she will be ceremonially clean again after her bleeding at childbirth. These are the instructions for a woman after the birth of a son or daughter.

Leviticus 12:6-7 NLT

_____

_____

_____

We now know why Mary and Joseph were at the temple, so let's set the scene for what is about to happen. They have come to the temple to offer their purification sacrifice. Luke tells us they offered birds instead of a lamb. Because of this, it is believed that Joseph and Mary were from a poor to moderate socio-economic background.

Let's imagine the proud parents bringing Jesus to the temple.

"Mary, it's okay. Don't be nervous. Everything will be fine." Joseph touched Mary's shoulder as they stood waiting on their turn to enter the temple. "Remember, many mothers have been in your sandals."

"Yes, I know they have, but this is my first time." Mary cuddled baby Jesus and gently rocked Him hoping His cries would quiet down before it was their turn to step forward.

What happened next was just the beginning of many signs and wonders throughout Jesus' lifetime.

Read Luke 2:36-38 again and write the story of Anna the prophetess in your own words.

> *Anna, a prophet, was also there in the Temple. She was the daughter of Phanuel from the tribe of Asher, and she was very old. Her husband died when they had been married only seven years. Then she lived as a widow to the age of eighty-four. She never left the Temple but stayed there day and night, worshiping God with fasting and prayer. She came along just as Simeon was talking with Mary and Joseph, and she began praising God. She talked about the child to everyone who had been waiting expectantly for God to rescue Jerusalem.*
>
> *Luke 2:36-38 NLT*

_____

_____

_____

_____

_____

What an inspiration Anna can be to us. Some versions say that Anna was a widow for eighty-four years. Let's do the math. If this was the case how old would Anna have been when Jesus was born? First, if she married at twelve years of age and was married for seven years, she would have been nineteen or twenty when her husband died. **Now add on the 84 years since her husband's death—how old would Anna have been when she met him in the Temple?**

_____

_____

_____

_____

There are lessons to be learned from Anna. The one that stands out to me is how Anna worshiped in the waiting. So much of our lives are spent waiting—waiting for our dreams to come to fruition; waiting for the results of a biopsy; waiting for our children to grow into young adults; waiting for a planned trip; and most of all, waiting for Jesus to return.

Whether it be for a few days or a few years, we will spend many hours of our lives waiting. While studying Anna, it dawned on me that she didn't just wait—she worshiped while she was waiting on the promised Savior. As we can see in the above verses from Luke, Anna never left the temple and spent her days fasting and praying during the waiting. Are there lessons to be learned from Anna? You bet! Let's look at one of those lessons.

NEVER GIVE UP

Have there ever been times when you wanted to give up? I don't have enough fingers to count how many times I've grown world-weary and wanted to throw in the towel. Well, maybe I have enough fingers for one day. As I have said many times, God's timing is not always our timing. I am amazed in my own life how circumstances changed with time. Trials I thought would never end were turned around and used for God's glory. He can do that!

For instance, my first book wasn't published until I was fifty-seven years old. Did you hear that, ladies? I was almost sixty! I remember a time in my forties when I was in the depths of despair and believed I wouldn't see fifty—I was physically and emotionally broken. But…God! I can't say I fasted and prayed every day while waiting, but I did keep putting one foot in front of the other, never losing sight of God.

Anna fasted and prayed during the waiting. Can you list five things you could do while in the waiting?

_____

_____

_____

_____

_____

_____

Let's decide today, beginning right now, to strive to be an Anna. And that includes me!

Chapter Two

MARY & MARTHA

Choose To Be Overwhelmed. Say What?

CHRISTINE TRIMPE

*"Martha, Martha," the Lord answered, "you are worried
and upset about many things, but few things are
needed—or indeed only one. Mary has chosen what is
better, and it will not be taken away from her."*
LUKE 10:41-42 NIV

Shortly before I turned fifty, I recall the Lord's whisper, "Stop
being so comfortable in your financially secure corporate career."
That came out of nowhere! Honestly, I was perfectly content in my
comfy corporate career, thank you very much.

Looking back, I clearly see that the Lord prepared me for something very different in my seasoned years. Long story short, I never
wanted to put myself out there to share the Gospel with others.
Still, after a dramatic weight loss journey and a restoration of my
body, mind, and spiritual health—God called me to serve. He has
a plan for you, too.

But where to begin when you're called by God? Let's glean
wisdom from the story of two sisters, Martha and Mary, in
Luke 10:38-42 NIV

As the story opens, Jesus visits while Martha is distracted preparing for visitors. Imagine her to-do list! Can you feel her angst and anxiety build as she sees her sister sitting at the Lord's feet? Martha might get a bad rap for her role in this story, but I see great wisdom in Martha's decision to take her concerns directly to Jesus.

When she does, Jesus gently rebukes her, saying, *"Martha, Martha," the Lord said, "you are worried and upset about many things, but few things are needed, or indeed only one. Mary has chosen what is better, and it will not be taken away from her"* (Luke 10:41-42 NIV).

Consider the distractions that hold you back or prevent you from serving God. I bet we can all relate to both sisters. On the one hand, the preparations must be done; on the other, Jesus instructs us to choose what is better.

How can God move us from distraction to devotion? Devotion in the way that Mary slowed down and sat at Jesus' feet to develop a deeper intimacy with God. Because, dear seasoned sister, this is where and when we hear His voice, like the whisper I heard concerning my future.

The best choice, as Jesus says, is to remove distractions and sit at His feet! It sounds so simple, but it's true that when we are overwhelmed, overworked, and out of time, somehow, it always seems to be the last thing on our checklist. And how often is it neglected?

Here's a helpful list to help you sit at His feet using the acronym ABIDE.

A: Appointment. Carve space in your day to sit at His feet.

B: Bible. There is nothing like a Bible to hold in your hand and write in the margins.

I: Intentional. Clear away distractions and dedicate this time to be alone with the Lord.

D: Devotional. A theologically sound Devotional or Bible study can provide extra insight.

E. Exalt. Spend time praising God!

Marthas, before long, this new discipline will be your daily delight. And Marys, since you already sit with Jesus daily, ask Him to give you a more profound passion for His Word to serve Him well.

Like me, you may be called into the most unexpected ways to serve God. Undoubtedly, the only thing that prepared me for this new season of ministry life was through spending time every morning in His Word. Together, we will all find great joy in seeking God in His Word to equip us to share the good news of what the Lord has done for you and me!

Application Questions:

Are you a Martha or a Mary, or a mixture of both? How do you balance the push-pull of devotion vs action?

Prayer:

Abba, help me discern when I need to be a Mary or when I need to be a Martha. I feel the daily distractions pulling at me and yet I want to be like Mary and spend time at your feet. Please show me the way to discern between these calls. Amen.

Christine Trimpe is an award-winning author, speaker, joy seeker, weight-loss warrior, and founder of The SugarFreed Me Weight Loss Solution.

Christine invites audiences to experience, embrace, and exclaim the joy of the Lord despite the weight of their circumstances. God's Word satisfies every craving—body, mind, and spirit! You can connect with Christine at www.christinetrimpe.com.

Where Are You God? I Need You Now!

DEBRA LYNN COLLINS

Trust in the Lord with all thine heart and lean not unto thine own understanding. In all thy ways acknowledge Him, and He shall direct thy paths.
PROVERBS 3:5-6 NKJV

Many times in my life, I have called out these very words to God. On my knees, tears streaming down my face, and heartbroken. Wondering where God was when I needed Him the most. All my dreams were shattered. I couldn't see the end of my pain and felt all alone. I couldn't understand why God didn't come running to my rescue when I called out to Him, "Where are you, God? I need you now."

This makes me think about the story of Mary and Martha. They faced this same pain when their brother, Lazarus, died.

The story of Mary & Martha in John 11:1-44 is a story of two sisters and their brother Lazarus, whom Jesus also loved. This Mary is the same one who washed Jesus' feet and dried them with her hair. What a way to show Jesus how much she loved Him. Then the day came when Lazarus became very sick, but his sisters knew exactly what to do. They had no doubt that if they could reach Jesus, He would come quickly, and their brother wouldn't die.

However, after Jesus received the news that Lazarus was sick, He stayed away two more days. During that time, Lazarus died. The sisters were heartbroken, and they felt like all hope was gone. Lazarus was dead. Nothing more could be done now. It was over.

"*Trust in the Lord with ALL thine heart.*" Trusting in God with all our hearts means we must trust God to the core of our being.

Even when we don't feel Him.

Even when we feel all alone and hopeless.

Even when we feel like our prayers are bouncing right back into our laps.

Trust God, even when it doesn't make sense.

Once Jesus reached Bethany, Lazarus had been dead for four days. Each sister told Jesus, "*If you had only been here, our brother would not have died.*" Through their grief, tears, and sorrows, Jesus was about to show Martha and Mary who He was and how much He loved them and their brother.

Jesus asked Mary, "*Where have you laid him?*" When they led Him to Lazarus's grave, Jesus said, 'Take away the stone.'"

Surprised, Martha replied, "*But Lord, he's been dead for four days; by now, he stinks.*"

Jesus said to her, "*Didn't I say to you, if you just believe, thou shall see the glory of God?*"

When they took away the stone from the cave, Jesus cried with a loud voice. "*Lazarus, come forth.*"

At His words, Lazarus came forth. Then Jesus said, "*Free him from the grave clothes and let him go.*"

When we put all our trust in the Lord, miracles happen. This shows us that God is still there even when we are at our lowest moments in life. He said He would never leave us nor forsake us.

Even during Mary and Martha's doubts, He still loved them and gave them a miracle. Don't you know those sisters' faith was made stronger than ever when Lazarus came out of that tomb?

God can still use us, too, even when our faith is weak. I've been there so many times. I'd be battling something, and someone would call me for prayer. Before I knew it, I'd find myself praying for them when I couldn't even pray for myself. In my darkest hour, God used me to help another along the way.

Application Questions:

How can you trust God, even though your situation seems bleak? What can you do to build your faith even when you doubt His plans?

Prayer:

Father God there is nothing more amazing to me than Your love. I know I can always count on You to help me when my doubts and fears try to overtake me. Thank you for always being at the frontline of every battle that I face. I put all my trust and hope in You. Amen.

Debra Lynn Collins is an Amazon Number One bestselling, self-published author. Her debut novel has sold over 200,000 copies since it was first published in August 2014. God has blessed Debra with four children, ten grandchildren, and soon-to-be four great-grandchildren. Through the years, she has tried her hand at many different crafts. She now owns her own small crafting business.

She is living her own happily-ever-after ending, in the state of Georgia, with her biggest fan, real-life hero, and husband, Steve, while writing contemporary Christian romances. She and her husband are also the pastors of their church in Lyerly, Georgia. Debra is a graduate from The Long Ridge Writers Group and an active member of American Christian Fiction Writers. You can connect with Debra at www.debralynncollins.com.

What Are You Doing?

LISA NELSON

But Martha was distracted by the big dinner she was preparing. She came to Jesus and said, "Lord, doesn't it seem unfair to you that my sister just sits here while I do all the work? Tell her to come and help me."

LUKE 10:40

"I feel like I should be doing more; I'm not doing enough."

"I wish I could do more."

"People will think I'm lazy or don't want to serve God if I don't do more."

These thoughts have passed through my mind on more than one occasion. Can you relate? As women, I think it's natural for us to feel like we should be "doing" something regularly. When we think of "doing," we tend to think of activities involving physical effort. As we age and our physical capacity becomes increasingly limited, it's easy to assume we have outlived our usefulness to Him because we can no longer "do" the things we used to do. Nothing could be further from the truth.

Although we don't know how old sisters Mary and Martha were at the time of our introduction to them in Luke's gospel account, there is still much for us to learn, regardless of our age and/or circumstances.

The story of Mary and Martha is a familiar one. If we're not careful, we can allow this familiarity to lull us into thinking we already know the "lesson" or the moral of the story. We know Jesus has arrived at the home of the sisters in Bethany. Upon His arrival, Martha immediately begins preparations for dinner, as any good hostess would do. I probably don't need to tell you what happens next, but if you need to refresh your memory, you can read it in Luke 10:38-40. The bottom line is that by all appearances, Mary is doing "nothing" while Martha busies herself with the practical tasks of dinner preparation. However, though Martha appears to be "doing" more, according to Jesus, she's not doing what is best or most important, depending on your Bible translation.

What does this story mean for those of us in our "winter" season? Though it's easy for us to come to a point where we feel less useful, Jesus delivers an important reminder: "You are worried and upset about many things, but only one thing is needed." This "one thing" is not found in our "busyness." It is found at the feet of Jesus. Thankfully, we never "age out" of the privilege, and even our physical limitations cannot keep us from this practice. Sometimes the most valuable thing we can do requires the least amount of effort. We can choose worship over work.

So, instead of letting the enemy try to convince us we must "do" more for our efforts to be effective for the Kingdom, let us instead remember the most effective investment of our time is to spend it with Him.

Application Questions:

Can you think of a time when you felt ineffective or useless to God because you couldn't physically participate in a ministry effort? Are there other ways you could support the ministry besides performing physical tasks? What are some examples of these types of (non-physical) tasks, and why are they also important?

Prayer:

Father God, teach us to know with certainty we can never outlive our usefulness to You. Give us the humility to remember our time is never wasted when we sit at the feet of Jesus. Teach us the virtue of "stillness," and give us the wisdom to know stillness in Your presence is not idleness or laziness but is a place from which we can draw strength and wisdom. May our hearts always be open to following wherever You lead. In Jesus' name. Amen.

Lisa Nelson is a mother to two incredibly talented young adults. Before becoming a full-time mom, she taught high school social studies and coached basketball and softball. She enjoys musical theatre, Atlanta Braves baseball and The West Wing when not watching her children perform. Lisa lives in Northwest Georgia with Jason, her husband of 26 years. Her raw and honest account in *My Season on the Bench: A Faith Empowered Quest to Get Back in the Game*, highlights her most powerful as well as her weakest moments that demonstrate her consistent faith in God. You can connect with Lisa at lhnelson68@gmail.com.

Distractibility. Are You Disctractable?

STEPHANIE RODDA

But Martha was distracted by the
big dinner she was preparing...
LUKE 10:40 NLT

So often, I can relate to Martha. Like her, I become distracted by everything that needs doing.

Martha is commonly epitomized as the sister who refused to be still and spend time at the feet of Jesus. I wonder if we misjudge her because we don't carefully consider the circumstances.

She obviously had the gift of hospitality, as the Bible clearly says she welcomed Jesus into her home. She seems to have been in a close relationship with the Lord as she freely expressed her feelings to Him. She apparently was important enough to Him to be heard, answered, and called by name.

> *But the Lord said to her, "My dear Martha, you are*
> *worried and upset over all these details!"*
>
> *Luke 10:41 NLT*

I regret to admit this often describes my state of mind. Worried and upset.

We live in a world that seems to applaud those who are busy. The busier, the better. It's as if being busy equals progress and ensures success. But, of course, this is not necessarily the case.

We seem to have lost the art of undivided attention. With so many demands on us, it's easy to feel pulled in every direction and tempted to juggle too many balls at a time. This can lead to weariness of the soul, and a few dropped balls.

Regardless of what frustrates our efforts to stay focused, we may feel responsible for doing it all, doing it all right now, and doing it all ourselves. In our early years, we may have promised ourselves that in the later years we'd be less distracted, less hurried, and certainly less flustered. And yet, now that we have arrived at this place in life where we are more "seasoned," we may feel overwhelmed with all that still needs doing.

Spiritual discipline is a practice that leads to spiritual strength, growth, and maturity. I believe it is a spiritual discipline to stay focused on what really matters. So, what does really matter?

Sometimes, what matters the most may seem to be completing the task at hand like Martha's meal preparations. But without exception, what always matters is being attentive to the presence of God and being willing to be still and listen despite our many duties.

Jesus did not chastise Martha for serving. Instead, he pointed out she was "worried and upset" and being distracted. We are, in fact, expected to stay busy with the Father's business.

If, however, we are so busy, so distracted by our works, that we can't be bothered to stop, be still, and listen to the Savior, our distractibility has become an obstacle.

> *"So, you see, faith by itself isn't enough. Unless it produces good deeds, it is dead and useless."*
>
> *James 2:17 NLT*

Application Questions:

As we considered Martha today, what did the Holy Spirit reveal that might be a hindrance, a distraction in your life? What spiritual discipline can you commit to that will prevent this recurrence?

Prayer:

Father, I know You love me just the way I am and yet, will not leave me as You find me. Thank you! Please remind me to stay attentive to Your presence and to keep the main thing, the very thing I focus on. Amen.

Stephanie Rodda is the wife of her one and only, mom of many, and GiGi to a growing number of grandchildren. She writes from her heart with the hopes of touching the souls of other women with words of encouragement. You can connect with Stephanie at www.stephanierodda.wordpress.com.

Mary & Martha

"Jesus! Can you believe I'm working like a slave to prepare a nice meal, and Mary's just sitting there doing nothing? Tell her to get up and come help me." Martha stands with feet apart and hands firmly planted on her hips, glaring at Mary.

Jesus didn't chastise Martha but spoke gently to her. "Martha, Martha. I understand that you have a lot of things on your mind right now. You are worried about making our meal just right. And that is a noble thing. But these are just details and not the most important thing right now. Mary has chosen the most important thing—to be with me and give me her full attention."

We can only imagine what happens next. Does Martha say something like, "Well, I never!" and huff off, or does Jesus' gentle rebuke cause her to pause, catch her breath, and realize she has lost sight of what is important?

Read Luke 10:38-42 and summarize the story of Martha and Mary. What were your first thoughts when you read this account?

_____

_____

_____

_____

_____

_____

_____

_____

_____

Our focus for this Bible Study is on women's worth in general and, more importantly, ways God can use us even in our winter season. But we will be studying women of all ages, backgrounds, and social standing. I know sometimes we tend to let wounds from our past affect who we are today, and then we question our usefulness as God's followers.

The exciting thing is we are going to discover God's love for women and how he can and will use us from childhood until death. My prayer is that by the time you finish this study, you will have discovered or rediscovered your worth during your winter season because if we live long enough, we will all have to go through our winter season. We are going to study a myriad of ways we can be useful even if we are not the young chicks we used to be.

Now, back to our discussion of Mary and Martha. I don't know about you, but there've been times when I would get all the Marys in the New Testament mixed up. I want us to take a little detour here to learn who Mary of Bethany is and who she isn't. Mary Magdalene and Mary of Bethany are two different women. And many times, Mary of Bethany is confused with the woman (with many sins) who anointed Jesus' feet with oil and her tears. We will discover there are two separate incidences when Jesus' feet were anointed with oil.

Luke introduces us to Mary of Magdala in Chapter 8.

Soon afterward Jesus began a tour of the nearby town and villages, preaching and announcing the Good News about the Kingdom of God. He took his twelve disciples with him, along with some women who had been cured of evil spirits and diseases. Among them were Mary Magdalene, from whom he had cast out seven demons; Joanna, the wife of Chuza, Herod's business manager; Susanna; and many others who were contributing from their own resources to support Jesus and his disciples.

Luke 8:1-3 NLT

This Mary, a faithful follower of Jesus, is frequently associated with the title "a woman of ill repute." This has been debated by scholars for many centuries, but there is no indication that she was ever a harlot.

Mary of Magdala has other distinctions as well. After reading Mark 15:39-41 write down where Mary was in this passage.

When the Roman officer who stood facing him saw how he had died, he exclaimed, "This man truly was the Son of God." Some women were there, watching from a distance, including Mary Magdalene, Mary (the mother of James the younger and Joseph), and Salome. They had been followers of Jesus and had cared for him while he was in Galilee. Many other women who had come with him to Jerusalem were also there.

Mark 15:39-41 NLT

_____

_____

_____

Read John 20:11-16.

Mary was standing outside the tomb crying, and as she wept, she stooped and looked in. She saw two white-robed angels, one sitting at the head and the other at the foot of the place where the body of Jesus had been lying. "Dear woman, why are you crying?" the angels asked her. "Because they have taken away my Lord," she replied, "and I don't know where they have put him." She turned to leave and saw someone standing there. It was Jesus, but she didn't recognize him. "Dear woman, why are you crying?" Jesus asked her. "Who are you looking for?" She thought he was the gardener. "Sir," she said, "if you have taken him away, tell me where you have put him, and I will go and get him." "Mary!" Jesus said. She turned to him and cried out, Rabboni!" (which is Hebrew for Teacher).

John 20:11-16 NLT

Describe what happened in this scene. Who did Jesus first appear to after the resurrection?

_____

_____

_____

_____

_____

_____

_____

_____

When I read this story it gives me chills—I can just see Mary desperately looking for Jesus. And she was rewarded for seeking him. As we can see through studying Mary Magdalene, she was one of

Jesus' faithful followers. Mary, a woman, was given the honor of being the first to see him after the resurrection.

There is another woman in the New Testament that many confuse with Mary Magdalene. We find her being introduced by Luke in chapter 7:36-38.

One of the Pharisees asked Jesus to have dinner with him, so Jesus went to his home and sat down to eat. When a certain immoral woman from the city heard he was eating there, she brought a beautiful alabaster jar filled with expensive perfume. Then she knelt behind him at his feet, weeping. Her tears fell on his feet, and she wiped them with her hair. Then she kept kissing his feet and putting perfume on them.

Luke 7:36-38 NLT

Continue reading through verse 50 in Chapter 7. Summarize what happened in the rest of this account.

_____

_____

_____

_____

_____

_____

_____

_____

This woman's name is not mentioned—only that she was a sinner. Going back and reading Luke's account in verses 18-23, we can see John the Baptist was still alive. So, this would have been early on in Jesus' ministry.

I love this account of John the Baptist. Even though he fully believed Jesus was the Messiah in his heart—his head just couldn't wrap around such miraculous events. He even asked his disciples to go ask Jesus, *"Are you the Messiah we've been expecting, or should we keep looking for someone else?"* (Luke 7:20 NLT).

Be sure and read further to discover the message Jesus sent back to John the Baptist. Okay, we took a little detour on our journey, but to me, this is an essential part of learning about the different Marys who are sometimes confused with each other.

Many centuries ago, scholars decided that this must be Mary Magdalene even though there is no indication it was her. Therefore, Mary was given the reputation of being a harlot—even when we don't know what her sins were.

This woman in Luke 7 may also be confused with Mary the sister of Martha and Lazarus. Let's dig a little deeper to find out why. This Mary (of Bethany) has also been thought to be the same Mary from Magdala. Here again, there is no indication that they were one and the same.

Let's look at the incident that tied these Marys together. Let's read John 12:1-3 together.

> *Six days before the Passover celebration began, Jesus arrived in Bethany, the home of Lazarus—the man he raised from the dead. A dinner was prepared in Jesus' honor. Martha served and Lazarus was among those who ate with him. Then Mary took a twelve-ounce jar of perfume made from the essence of nard, and she anointed Jesus' feet with it. The house was filled with the fragrance.*
>
> *John 12:1-3 NLT*

Let's note some of the differences in the story from Luke.

When did this dinner take place?

_____

_____

Who was present during the meal?

_____

_____

Who took the jar of perfume and anointed Jesus' feet?

_____

_____

After comparing the two encounters with Jesus can you list some of the differences in these two stories?

_____

_____

_____

In John's account of this meal, we begin to see the personalities of Mary and Martha emerge. Reread John 12:1-3 and answer the following questions.

What is Martha doing?

_____

_____

_____

What is Mary doing?

_____

_____

_____

What differences do you see emerging between these two women?

_____

_____

_____

_____

_____

_____

I love the way Edith Deen describes them in her book, *All of the Women of the Bible.*

> While Martha was practical and unemotional, Mary was impassioned and imaginative. Martha probably was the older and mothered Mary; and she took the lead as a home-maker. Probably Martha was a widow and Mary never married. Despite their differences, Martha and Mary exhibited a close bond of sympathy for each other.
>
> Like most attentive, eager-hearted, and affectionate hostesses, Martha strove for perfection around her house, especially when a guest the family loved as much as they did when Jesus came for a visit. Mary was more pensive and the quieter of the two. As Martha bustled about her home duties, she did not have Mary's calmness or her holy trustfulness.

Can you relate to this? I know I can. From birth my daughters had personalities as different as night and day. My oldest daughter Erin would stay in the yard, and I never had to worry about her darting into the road. Now my youngest daughter, Niki, was a little more precocious. For instance, one day I got a call from our neighbor telling me Niki was in her yard across the street. All that time, I had thought she was in the house. After that incident, we had a fence installed so we could keep her corralled in the yard where she would be safe. There is absolutely nothing wrong with either of these personalities and it is the same in Mary and Martha's case.

Write down an example (Biblical or personal) you can think of that might represent Mary and Martha.

_____

_____

_____

_____

_____

_____

Sometimes I think Martha gets a bad rap. But there is absolutely nothing wrong with what Martha was trying to accomplish. I am very much a Martha. My mother had severe Rheumatoid Arthritis, and I had to take on a lot of household responsibilities as a young child. This left me with a feeling of having to get the job done, and make sure everything was perfect.

This sense of responsibility followed me into adulthood. I've had to strive in my winter season to incorporate some of Mary into me. I try to take some time in the morning to spend with God. I don't always follow the same routine every day. Some days, I miss my quiet time completely. As Stephanie Rodda said in her devotion, we probably dreamed of our winter season and pictured it as a calm, restful time. But most of us still have busy lives, and this busyness can get in the way of our spending time at the feet of God.

Do you consider yourself a Mary or a Martha, or a combination of both? What are some ways you can think of where you can sit at the feet of Jesus and try to rid your life of ineffective busyness?

I encourage you to embark on your own digging expedition and delve deeper into the lives of Mary and Martha. You will find differences in their personalities, but one thing they had in common was their love for Christ and their faith in Him as their Savior.

Let's look at John 11:23-27 to discover that Martha had the privilege of testifying to Jesus' being our Messiah. What great faith she possessed.

> *Jesus told her, "Your brother will rise again." "Yes, Martha said, "he will rise when everyone rises, at the last day." Jesus told her, "I am the resurrection and the life. Anyone who believes in me will live, even after dying. Everyone who lives in me and believes in me will never, ever die. Do you believe this, Martha?" "Yes, Lord," she told him. "I have always believed you are the Messiah, the Son of God, the one who has come into the world from God."*
>
> *John 11:23-27 NLT*

After reading this scripture write what Jesus asks Martha and then write Martha's reply. Do you believe this declaration highlights Martha's boldness and faith?

_____

_____

_____

_____

_____

_____

I love this scripture. Martha took that grit and determination she possessed and turned it around to profess Jesus is the Messiah. And it was after this confession that Jesus raised Lazarus from the dead. Let's all strive to be a combination of Mary and Martha—two faithful women who loved Jesus. If you tend to be a little more like Martha than Mary, your winter season is the perfect time to give yourself permission to sit at the feet of Jesus!

Chapter Three

MARY & ELIZABETH

Unpack Those Bags

JANICE THOMPSON

"Therefore, my beloved brothers, be steadfast, immovable, always abounding in the work of the Lord, knowing that in the Lord your labor is not in vain."
1 CORINTHIANS 15:58 ESV

Pack your bags, sister. Your best days are behind you.

Have you ever struggled with negative mind-chatter like the phrase above? I have. As I've tip-toed over the threshold into my golden years, I've questioned my usefulness—to my family, church, and community. Hello out there! Does anyone have use for an old gal like me, or is there an expiration date stamped on my forehead?

At times, self-doubts related to my age and health cause me to freeze up. I don't make myself available to others as readily as I used to. I wonder if the younger ones will roll their eyes and whisper, "It's that old lady again, trying to weasel her way in. Would someone please tell her she's no longer needed or wanted?"

No doubt Elizabeth felt the same way. Though she had enjoyed many wonderful years of marriage to the priest Zechariah, Elizabeth was now well past her childbearing years. Oh, she was a dedicated and faithful woman from a priestly line herself. But without a child to show from her union with Zechariah, she no doubt felt useless and ostracized by society. Elizabeth heard the whispers. She saw pitying looks from the young mothers as they nursed their babes and tended to their little ones.

I can't even imagine the shock, or delight? Disbelief? Confusion? when the elderly Elizabeth received the news that she would deliver a son. Finally, after all these years!

And what a son he was! John the Baptist would prepare the way for the Savior of the world, Jesus Christ. Through his birth, Elizabeth received the promise of 1 Peter 5: 6-7, even before the words were penned. *"Humble yourselves, therefore, under the mighty hand of God so that at the proper time he may exalt you, casting all your anxieties on him, because he cares for you"* (ESV).

Elizabeth's cousin, Mary came for a visit not long after receiving her own big news that she would birth the savior into the world. What a fascinating few months they must have shared, as the elderly Elizabeth and her teenage cousin, Mary, went through their pregnancies together. These two vastly different women suddenly had everything in common. I can only imagine the conversations they must have had! And talk about cravings! Pickled herring, anyone?

Picture yourself in Elizabeth's shoes. Maybe you've felt overlooked, left out, and past your prime. Or perhaps you're like Mary, feeling too young to tackle life's problems.

Here's the good news: God can and will use you if you submit yourself to Him and wait patiently to fulfill His promises.

Together, Mary and Elizabeth embodied the rock-solid truth found in Romans 8:28. *"And we know that for those who love God, all things work together for good, for those who are called according to his purpose"* (ESV).

He will work them for good in your life, too. So don't pack those bags quite yet, sweet woman of God. He's got plenty of good roads ahead for you.

Application Questions:

Have you ever used your age as an excuse not to step out in faith? How will Elizabeth's or Mary's examples inspire you to trust God?

Prayer:

Lord, thank you for finding me usable, no matter my age. I won't pack my bags just yet. You've got a lot of great things in store for me and I'm so grateful. Amen.

Janice Thompson is a Christian author who lives in Spring, Texas. She has published a variety of novels and non-fiction books for the Christian market. These days Janice can be found in the kitchen, baking for her recipe blog, www.outoftheboxbaking.com. To learn more about her books, visit her website at www.janiceathompson.com.

Are We Ever Too Young... Or Too Old?

KATHI MACIAS

*And it happened, when Elizabeth heard the greeting
of Mary, that the babe leaped in her womb; and
Elizabeth was filled with the Holy Spirit.*
LUKE 1:41 NKJV

We are never too old—or too young—to be part of a miracle. I wasn't aware of that when I became a Christian at the age of twenty-six. Though I immediately got involved in a good church with numerous ministry opportunities, I felt unqualified to volunteer for any of them. Not only was I relatively young in years, but I was also a brand-new Christian. Now, nearly fifty years later, I sometimes must fight the feeling that I'm too old to be useful to God. However, according to the Bible, I was wrong on both counts because God can use us at any age—if we have a willing heart.

No one exemplifies that powerful truth better than a pair of Jewish cousins, Mary and Elizabeth. Elizabeth is barren and beyond childbearing years when we first meet her in Luke 1. Though she and her husband, Zacharias, worshiped and served God faithfully, Elizabeth had never been able to have a child. In the culture of the day, that was considered a curse. No doubt, the elderly couple had long since given up on ever welcoming a child into their home. Then God sent an angel to announce to Zacharias that Elizabeth would indeed bear a child, a son who would prepare the way for the Messiah.

A few months later, the angel Gabriel appeared to a young Jewish girl named Mary. He told her she would soon have a baby who would be called the Son of the Highest. Because she was a virgin, Mary questioned how that was possible. Gabriel explained to her that the power of the Highest would overshadow her, and her child would be called the Son of God. This faithful, humble young woman immediately declared, *"Behold the maidservant of the Lord! Let it be to me according to your word..."* (Luke 1:38 NKJV).

How many of us—regardless of age or length of time as a Christian—would respond so quickly and humbly? I would like to think I would, but I am painfully aware of far too many times when I've questioned God over far less miraculous situations than anything Mary or Elizabeth were promised. And yet, God has blessed us all with so many promises throughout the Scriptures, including Jeremiah 29:11, which declares, *"For I know the thoughts that I think toward you," says the Lord, "thoughts of peace and not of evil, to give you a future and a hope."*

God's plans and promises for us are better than anything we could ever imagine or fulfill on our own. Will we, like Mary and Elizabeth, submit our future to God and trust Him to do as He has promised? If so, we will soon find ourselves in places of service we can only describe as miraculous.

When God calls us to a new area of ministry, we need only remember that He will actually do the work, though He graciously allows us to be the vessels for that work to take place. *"He who calls you is faithful, who also will do it"* (1 Thessalonians 5:24 NKJV).

Application Questions:

Has God ever called you to a place of service that you knew you couldn't perform on your own? How did God enable you to do it?

Prayer:

Father, God, the longer I walk with You, the more I realize my utter and complete dependence on You for every area of my life. Whether the remainder of my life here on earth will be measured in years or days, I ask that You use me every day for Your glory until I am safely home with You. In Jesus' mighty name, Amen.

Kathi Macias (kathimacias.com) is a best-selling author of nearly 60 books, as well as a popular speaker at writers' conferences and women's events. She and her husband, Al, live in Southern California where they enjoy spending time with their children, grandchildren, and great-grandchildren.

Take A Chance On God. Again.

PATRICIA DURGIN

Why, my soul, are you downcast? Why so disturbed within me? Put your hope in God, for I will yet praise him, my Savior and my God.
PSALMS 42:5 NIV

"We're leaving for Thailand next Saturday," our younger daughter Kristen said. She and our son-in-love Patrick had prayed for and planned this trip for three years. They would serve the poorest of the poor high on a mountain with no modern luxuries such as running water.

As fellow believers, my husband David and I were thrilled. We reared our two daughters to follow Christ wherever He led. As parents, we prayed for Him to keep them safe, aware that might not be His plan. What would their obedience to God cost them? We didn't know.

Mary, the mother of Jesus, and Elizabeth, the mother of John the Baptist, surely prayed diligently for their miracle children even while carrying them.

Mary bore Jesus at a young age. Elizabeth, older, bore John past the usual childbearing age. Both infants were gifts from God. Their parents knew it. How they must have dreamed of His plans for their precious baby boys.

As Jesus and John matured, both women realized their sons' calling—to proclaim God's Good News—was more than dangerous. It might cost them their lives. Years later, it did.

What's it like to watch your child sacrificially obey Christ only to be hated, threatened, and eventually killed by those who claim allegiance to the same God? I pray you and I never know. But Mary and Elizabeth knew.

We're told little about Elizabeth's life after Herod ordered John beheaded.

Mary was part of Jesus' ministry and continued to serve after His resurrection. Whether a young girl or old woman, Mary's age and gender were never stumbling blocks, even in a culture that typically didn't value women. God saw only her love and willingness to serve Him.

While on the cross, Christ illustrated how much He valued his mother, in John 19:25-27 NIV: *"Near the cross of Jesus stood his mother, his mother's sister, Mary the wife of Clopas, and Mary Magdalene. When Jesus saw his mother there, and the disciple whom he loved standing nearby, he said to her, 'Woman, here is your son,' and to the disciple, 'Here is your mother.' From that time on, this disciple took her into his home."*

She was also in attendance in the upper room after Christ's ascension, found in Acts 1:14 NIV: *"They all joined together constantly in prayer, along with the women and Mary the mother of Jesus, and with his brothers."*

We can learn so much from these two Godly women. They remained committed to God, even after losing their sons to His cause. Instead of rejecting Him, they turned to Him for healing.

God knows humans are weak. We want His guarantee that He'll require so much and no more of us and those we love. He makes no such pledge. Instead, He promises to be with us come what may. When all is well, we thank Him for that promise. But when disaster looms, we cling to it as we long more for His presence than His deliverance.

He kept His promises to Mary and Elizabeth. He keeps His promises to us, too. Our children returned from Thailand safe. Hallelujah!

> *…The LORD is trustworthy in all he promises and faithful in all he does.*
>
> *Psalms 145:13b NIV*

Application Questions:

*Is Christ calling you to step outside your comfort zone? He won't **send** you. He'll go **with** you. Praying you dare to take a chance on God. Again.*

Prayer:

Father, it's through our pain that we discover your faithfulness. Thank you for showering us with your comfort and peace. May we offer that same gift to others in your name, Amen.

Patricia Durgin has served Christian writers and speakers since 1999. As a marketing coach, she partners with her clients to shine His light through their message so clearly their audience can find them in the dark. Find out how she can help you at marketersonamission.com.

Ever Had A Day?

RITA PROCHAZKA

"And blessed is she who believed that there would be a
fulfillment of what was spoken to her from the Lord."
LUKE 1:45 ESV

Have you ever heard the expression, "It's been a day?" Recently a friend said that to me, and I knew immediately what she meant. It had been an exasperating day with twists and turns that left her wondering what would happen next.

As we read in the verses of Luke 1, Mary and Elizabeth's "day" was filled with joy, laughter, singing, and companionship. It was filled with praise to God, who had blessed them each with a miracle. One older, barren mother to birth the boy who would proclaim the One to come, and the young virgin mother who would give birth to the One to come, the long-awaited Messiah.

Can you imagine what they must have felt as they looked at each other, then at their stomachs, both showing signs of the children within?

How to explain the feelings, the mystery of it all.

But as women do, I think they also spoke of their other "It's been a day" experiences. Don't we recount the challenges before the good happens, trying in our hearts and minds to understand it all?

The months and years of Elizabeth's barrenness, her longing for a child, Zechariah becoming mute, and just out of nowhere, the long prayed for pregnancy after all that. Mary would have shared about the angel's appearance and her shock, wonder, and obedience that followed his proclamation. She wasn't married to Joseph yet, and the gossip was already being whispered around the neighborhood. Both women had their "day," and it had been a long one. All in preparation.

I've had my share of "it's been a day" experiences. Many, in fact. They have sometimes been as inconvenient as a flat tire, a burned dinner, or, more seriously, an ill child. One of my daughters battled health issues as a teen and was so ill I took her to the hospital. They kept her overnight for testing, and as I drove home, I cried, praying and entrusting her into God's hands and the hospital's care. My husband was out of the country, so I felt very alone, but I truly wasn't. We had God and each other. We grew stronger as we faced this obstacle in her life. That was "a day."

God knows about these days. They are in His plans for us. The day may not make sense. The day will come when we are young and when we are old. The day molds, shapes, refines, and makes us more like Christ. We are imperfect beings who need our perfect God. Even amid a challenging day, there is immense peace in our obedience to His call.

Mary and Elizabeth obediently walked where God had taken them—a journey neither thought they would ever experience. But when they did, they knew who to trust. As seasoned women, we should remember the days that stretched our faith and caused us to lean hard into Him. It was all for preparation. These days make us more like Christ. We should remember and celebrate the good days, the love-filled, fun days that are a gift from Him, the days that show us His unlimited love, so we can live with a heart of gratitude.

Application Questions:

How do you handle your day? Do you accept it with grace, gratitude, and humbleness before Him? Do you complain and gripe about the inconveniences?

Prayer:

Dear Lord, thank You for this "day." Enable me to find gratitude and grace in each moment and to remember You have a plan and a purpose for me through it all. In Jesus' name. Amen.

Rita's call to short-term mission trips has placed her in many unique places worldwide. She's writing a book highlighting her experiences and the people she's met in her ministry. Rita lives in Michigan with her husband, Mark. They have three children and four grandchildren. You can reach Rita at ritaprochazka73@gmail.com.

Mary (Mother Of Jesus) & Elizabeth

Read Luke Chapter 1 to prepare for Mary and Elizabeth's journey.

Darkness engulfs the little house where young Mary is sleeping. The only light visible is from the full moon overhead, peeking through her open window. Until…

Enter Stage Left! Gabriel appears!

> *"Don't be afraid Mary," the angel told her, "for you have found favor with God! You will conceive and give birth to a son, and you will name him Jesus. He will be great and will be called the Son of the Most High. The Lord God will give him the throne of his ancestor David. And he will reign over Israel forever, his Kingdom will never end!"*
>
> *Luke 1:30-33 NLT*

What news did the angel bring to young Mary? How do you think she reacted when she was awakened by the angel Gabriel?

_____

_____

_____

_____

_____

_____

To me, this is one of the most beautiful stories in the Bible. It is the story of our redemption—the beginning and the end. Through the obedience of this young girl—and she was most likely a mere teenager—our Savior is born. He lived thirty-three years on earth as a fully human being. Because of this, he has experienced every human emotion that we go through.

Let's read Hebrews 4:14-16.

> *So then, since we have a great High Priest who has entered heaven, Jesus the Son of God, let us hold firmly to what we believe. This High Priest of ours understands our weaknesses, for he faced all the same testings we do, yet he did not sin. So let us come boldly before the throne of our gracious God. There we will receive his mercy, and we will find grace to help us when we need it most.*
>
> *Hebrews 4:14-16*

Can you find other verses sharing the good news that Jesus is our intercessor? Write them down.

_____

_____

_____

_____

_____

_____

_____

As we travel this journey with Mary and Elizabeth, we'll begin to see how God used young and old to fulfill his promises. This is exciting news for us! And as we dig deeper into their backgrounds, we'll discover God did not choose royalty, the famous, or even the wealthy to bring his son into the world. He chose the "ordinary!" What great news for us.

I love how simply Max Lucado explains it in his book *Ten Women of the Bible*:

> They, are, well, normal. Normal means calluses like Joseph, stretch marks like Mary. Normal stays up late with laundry and wakes up early for work. Normal drives the car pool wearing a bathrobe and slippers. Normal is Norm and Norma, not Prince and Princess.
>
> Norm sings off-key. Norma works in a cubicle and struggles to find time to pray. Both have stood where Joseph stood and have heard what Mary heard. Not from the innkeeper in Bethlehem but from the coach in middle school or the hunk in high school or the foreman at the plant. We don't have room for you…time for you…a space for you…a job for you…interest in you. Besides, look at you. You are too slow…fat…inexperienced…late…young…old…pigeon-toed…cross-eyed…hackneyed. You are too…ordinary.
>
> But then comes the Christmas story—Norm and Norma from Normal, Ohio, plodding into the ho-hum Bethlehem in the middle of the night. No one notices them. No one looks twice in their direction. The innkeeper won't even clean out a corner in the attic. Trumpets don't blast, bells don't sound, and angels don't toss confetti. Aren't we glad they didn't?

Thank God he values "who we are" and not what we have! We find so many instances in the Bible that show how God and Jesus went out of their way to use others deemed "less than."

Put on your hiking boots, grab your hiking stick, and let's begin our journey back into the Old Testament. By now, you are tired, hot, and hungry and wondering why in the world is she taking me all the way back here. Don't give up!

Do you see him just up ahead? There's Samuel! The Lord has asked him to find a replacement for King Saul, who disobeyed God, thus losing his Kingdom in the process. Samuel arrived at the house of Jesse, where God told Samuel he would choose Saul's replacement from one of Jesse's sons.

> *When they arrived Samuel took one look at Eliab and thought, "Surely this is the Lord's anointed." But the Lord said to Samuel, "Don't judge by his appearance or height, for I have rejected him. The Lord doesn't see things the way you see them. People judge by outward appearance, but the Lord looks at the heart."*
>
> *1 Samuel 16:6-7 NLT*

Continue reading through verse 13. After reading the account of David, I felt plumb giddy. God doesn't look at the outside—he looks at our hearts. We can be young, old, fat, skinny, short, tall, or you can fill in the blanks. The Lord is more interested in our faithfulness to him instead of how pretty or handsome we are. And that is music to my ears.

After reading the account of how David was chosen, does this make you feel more confident that God can and will use you— even in your winter season? Why do you feel this way?

_____

_____

_____

Find other examples in the Old or New Testament where God or Jesus used less-than-perfect people for his ministry. Write them down and where you found them.

_____

_____

_____

_____

_____

_____

_____

_____

_____

_____

Okay, we've just gone on a rabbit trail, but I felt like it was very important for you to understand that God seeks out the unassuming, plain, unnoticed—the ordinary! He seeks us out for our passion, our love for Him, and our heart to share the good news with others. Praise God, I am ordinary.

After stopping for a break and quenching our thirst with much-needed water, we have arrived back in the New Testament where Mary has just been told she will be the mother of the world's Savior. When Gabriel appeared in a glow of light, I can only imagine how frightened she must have felt—maybe she even thought she was dreaming. But then Gabriel opened his mouth and spoke (I imagine his voice being like that of Dennis Haysbert, the All-State Insurance spokesman).

> *Confused and disturbed, Mary tried to think what the angel could mean. "Don't be afraid Mary," the angel told her, "for you have found favor with God. You will conceive*

and give birth to a son, and you will name him Jesus. He will be very great and will be called the Son of the Most High. The Lord God will give him the throne of his ancestor David. And he will reign over Israel forever, his Kingdom will never end!"

Luke 1:29-33 NLT

How do you think you might have reacted if you were in Mary's sandals? Would you have thought, "Why me? I'm just an ordinary girl." Write your answer below.

_____

_____

_____

_____

_____

_____

_____

_____

"Mother, I must go see Elizabeth. I need her wisdom, strength, and encouragement," Mary said to her mother.

"Yes, dear, I agree with you. Elizabeth would be thrilled to see you, and you will be able to spill out your heart to her," Mary's mother said.

It's hard to speak of Mary without speaking of her cousin Elizabeth. This is a perfect example of how we, as seasoned women, can spill our faith experiences into the heart of younger women. It's easy to picture young Mary being overwhelmed after being told she would become the mother of the world's Savior.

Not only was she going to be the mother of our Redeemer, but she was not married and knew there would be consequences to

bear when her news was discovered. She needed someone to talk
to. There have been many times when I've been overwhelmed with
life and wanted to run to the comfort of an older woman. Not
only could they offer comfort, but they had experienced life much
longer than I had and possessed the knowledge and wisdom that
comes with age. Now I am in that season.

This is what Edith Deen had to say about this beautiful relationship in her book, *All the Women of the Bible.*

> *During these three months that Mary visited Elizabeth, we can
> imagine that they unburdened their hearts to each other and
> that Elizabeth had many words of wisdom for Mary, who was
> young enough to be Elizabeth's daughter. Yet in their common
> experience of approaching motherhood the age difference became
> insignificant as they joyfully planned for the birth of their sons,
> who were to be so near the same age.*

**Write down a time when you ran to a seasoned woman for
comfort and wisdom. Do you think you could offer the same to
younger women now?**

_____
_____
_____
_____
_____

Elizabeth lived during the reign of Herod the Great, during
the time just before Jesus was born. She was the wife of a
temple priest, Zechariah. Devoutly religious, the two lived
in the hill country of Judea, in close proximity to Jerusalem,
where Zachariah ministered at the Temple from Sabbath

to Sabbath. Elizabeth means "God is my oath" or "a worshiper of God." Both these meanings are entirely fitting for a woman who proved she had eternal trust in the Lord, even in the face of a major setback—the inability to conceive a child. (*Women in the Bible For Dummies*)

Let me introduce you to this Godly couple.

When Herod was King of Judea, there was a Jewish priest named Zechariah. He was a member of the priestly order of Abijah, and his wife Elizabeth , was also from the priestly line of Aaron. Zachariah and Elizabeth were righteous in God's eyes, careful to obey all of the Lord's commandments and regulations. They had no children because Elizabeth was unable to conceive, and they were both very old.

Luke 1: 5-7 NLT

What can you tell us about Elizabeth from the passage above?

_____

_____

_____

_____

_____

_____

When the idea of writing this Bible study came to mind, I knew I wanted to encourage women over fifty (or younger, as some have been an "old soul" even from a young age) whom I lovingly refer to as seasoned women. I wanted to use examples of seasoned women in the Bible to show that God *can* and *will* use us even in our winter season.

But by no means did I plan on using only seasoned women to show us how much we can still give—no matter how big or how small. It can't be done without using women of all ages to help us see our worth. And Mary and Elizabeth are perfect examples of how God uses women of all ages for His glory.

Elizabeth's story comes to an end as John's story is just beginning. John's religious fervor is developed first through devout examples of his mother and father. And John's humility—reflected in his recognition that Jesus is divine and greater than he—is due certainly in part to Elizabeth's rearing. Remember, Elizabeth, the elder cousin, shows respect for Mary, who is carrying the Lord. Neither Elizabeth nor John the Baptist give any signs of jealousy. Mary stays with Elizabeth for three months until John is born and then returns home, three months pregnant with Jesus. (*Women in the Bible for Dummies*)

Write down Luke 1:56.

_____

_____

_____

_____

_____

_____

_____

_____

_____

_____

_____

_____

There is no more mention of Elizabeth after John's circumcision?

When the baby was eight days old, they all came for the circumcision ceremony. They wanted to name him Zachariah, after his father. But Elizabeth said, "No! His name is John!" "What?" they exclaimed. "There is no one in all your family by that name. So they used gestures to ask the baby's father what he wanted to name him. He motioned for a writing tablet, and to everyone's surprise he wrote, "His name is John." Instantly, Zechariah could speak again, and he began praising God.

Luke 1:59-64 NLT

What happened during the circumcision ceremony of John. Why was this conversation among friends and family so significant? (Read Luke 1)

_____

_____

_____

_____

_____

_____

_____

_____

_____

_____

Even though we don't have the full story of Elizabeth after John's birth, we know enough that she was a Godly influence on John. But, it is different with Mary. She followed Jesus throughout his ministry and was with him when he performed his first miracle, when he was crucified on the cross, and when he was raised from the tomb as our Savior Redeemer. But she didn't stop there. She continued to be supportive of the apostles. She spent her life supporting Jesus. From a young girl to a seasoned woman, she devoted her life to God. Are we willing to do the same?

Write down two or three verses where Mary supported her son. Can you think of ways you could be supportive during your winter season—no matter how big or small?

_____

_____

_____

_____

_____

_____

_____

_____

Chapter Four

LOIS & EUNICE

Can We Be a Generational Influence?

DELORES LIESNER

*"I have no greater joy than to hear that my
children are walking in the truth."*
3 John 1:4 ESV

"Four o'clock? As in a.m.?" I looked at my eleven-year-old
grandson and moaned. "We'll have to be up at four a.m.
every morning…for a year?"

The hard-to-get neighborhood paper route was open now.
If I took it for a year and trained my grandson, he could take it
over when he turned twelve. "I'll set my own alarm," he told his
parents. "And I'll be so quiet when I open the door for Gramma
every morning." I couldn't say no to those pleading puppy dog
eyes, nor could his parents. He cheered and grinned at me. "It's
only one year, Gramma!"

And so it began. Every morning we dragged huge bundles of
papers and plastic bags inside, then rolled, stuffed, and packed
them in two ginormous shoulder bags. We each took a side of
the street. There was a lot of cackling between us when a paper
missile would fly onto a porch roof or land in bushes, awaken-
ing a flock of birds. As part of the routine, we reviewed his Bible
verses for Awana. He would recite a part of the verse, and we'd say

the reference together. We were both amazed at how quickly we learned the verses. Our bagging time gave us the opportunity to discuss their life applications.

Lois, a Jewish believer, and her daughter, Eunice, had a similar generational link with the Apostle Paul's sidekick, Timothy. In 2 Timothy 1:5, Paul tells Timothy, "*I am reminded of your sincere faith, a faith that dwelt first in your grandmother Lois and your mother Eunice and now, I am sure, dwells in you as well.*" Lois was mentioned as a Jewess who believed, but her husband was Greek.

Like Lois and Eunice, many women today are the only believers in their households. Not an easy path, but, like our sisters of old, we have the same calling to teach children and grandchildren about Jesus Christ. Biblical families lived together in one home, so Timothy saw all sides of his family's personalities and sinful natures. Yet God worked mightily in that little family. As an adult, Timothy influenced thousands to turn to Christ. And it all began with the quiet but bold faith of a Jewish mom and grandma.

Lois and Eunice's faithfulness speaks to us today, reminding us to demonstrate our love for the Lord unashamedly. When you have opportunities to share your faith (with or without words) with your children and grandchildren, know that you might be influencing future generations!

Application Questions:

Have you told your children or grandchildren what God has done for you? How can you demonstrate the difference Christ makes in your life?

Prayer:

Heavenly Father, help me to walk, talk and live my faith before the generations that come after me. Let them see

that faith is a natural occurrence in a healthy relation-
ship with you, just as love is natural between them and
me. Help me to help them develop the habit of walking,
talking, and living with you. Amen.

Delores Liesner's passion, whether writing or speaking about activating faith is to be the miracle for others. She's published hundreds of stories and teachings online and in print including a dozen Chicken Soup books, and a devotional, *Be the Miracle!* You can contact her through DeloresLiesner.com.

On Whose Account?

LINDA KOZAR

Train up a child in the way he should go, and
when he is old, he shall not depart from it.
PROVERBS 22:6 NKJV

John Wesley said he learned more about Christianity from his mother than from all the theologians in England. This was also true of Timothy, the Apostle Paul's protégé who was raised by his devout mother Eunice and his grandmother Lois. Born of a Jewish mother and Greek father who perhaps passed away when he was a child, Timothy grew up under the tutelage of the two most influential women in his life, who assumed the responsibility for his instruction in Scripture and likely taught the boy from memory since scrolls were costly and books didn't exist.

Lois may have heard the gospel through the ministry of Paul and Barnabas on their first missionary journey to Derbe and Lystra in 48 CE. *"I am reminded of your sincere faith, a faith that dwelt first in your grandmother Lois and your mother Eunice and now, I am sure, dwells in you as well"* (2 Timothy 1:5). The women shared the gospel with him. Timothy matured into a young man of faith and wisdom with a deep understanding of both cultures and the profound ability to preach effectively to both. When Paul returned, the disciples there spoke well of the young man (Acts 16:1-4), so much so that Paul invited him to accompany him on his missionary journeys.

The women in Timothy's life invested devotion, fervent faith, and spiritual truth into their beloved son and grandson. Beyond scriptural instruction and the law of Moses and the prophets, Eunice and Lois illustrated their faithfulness to God by living what they believed. But the time had come for Timothy to grow further and go farther. Paul would continue where they left off, mentoring the young man he later regarded as his spiritual son. *"But as for you, continue in what you have learned and have firmly believed, knowing from whom you learned it"* (2 Timothy 3:14).

Godly mothers not only bring you up, but they also bring you to God.

Is there a mother or grandmother in your life who prays, encourages, and supports the younger generations in the faith? Godly women invest in a heavenly treasury of prayers and a heritage of faith for their loved ones. Praying mamas deposit a foundation of wisdom and understanding into their children's lives, building up their character and committing their future to God.

Application Questions:
Are you that woman of prayer and commitment who faithfully intercedes for your loved ones? If not, ask God to help you develop a stronger prayer life. Your family is your greatest God-given treasure and wealth beyond measure.

Prayer:
Dear Lord, please help me to sow into the lives of my grandchildren, and great-grandchildren, to teach them the fundamentals of life, of spiritual instruction from God's

Holy Word, and from a wealth of experience I have gained over the years. Let their minds be humble and open to instruction, to correction, and to hasten to the throne for the superior teaching of the Holy Spirit. In Jesus' name. Amen.

Linda Kozar is an award-winning multi-published author of traditional and indie-published fiction and nonfiction inspirational books. In 2022, *Sweet Tea for The Soul,* (DaySpring) received an ECPA Bronze Sales Award for 100,000+ copies sold. In 2021, *Sunshine for The Soul,* took home a First Place Selah and Nonfiction Book of the Year at the Blue Ridge Mountain Christian Writers Conference. She and her husband, Michael, married for 32 years, live in The Woodlands, Texas, enjoying spending time with their two grown daughters, their wonderful son-in-law, granddaughter Eden, and Gypsy, their rascally Jack Russell Terrier. NEW devotional release in April 2024, *Gimme Some Sugar* (Broadstreet Publishing). You can contact Linda at www.lindakozar.com.

Faith for the Generations

PATTY SMITH HALL

"I am reminded of your sincere faith,
which first lived in your grandmother Lois
and in your mother, Eunice, and, I am
persuaded, now lives in you also."
2 TIMOTHY 1:5

As I strapped my youngest grandson into his car seat for our weekly ride to church, a melancholy fell over my heart. Our son-in-law had recently been transferred to a town almost two hours away, which meant their family would be moving in the next few weeks. These Sunday morning rides to church would soon come to an end.

It breaks my grandmother's heart to think about it.

Though my daughter was raised in church and professes her belief in Jesus as her Savior, she is unchurched at this time. It hurts to hear the pain in her voice whenever she talks about her feelings toward the church. Because of this, I can only pray that one day, she'll forgive whatever happened and re-establish her relationship with Christ. That's why when our first grandson was born, I knew I'd have to be more active in his spiritual upbringing. Right before his second birthday, my grandson went to church with me for the first time. Three years later, his younger brother joined our little carpool to Sunday school.

Our church together doesn't stop there. On the way home, we discuss what they learned in Sunday school. My oldest grandson always has some great questions. Like when he was learning about Communion, and he asked, "Does God really make us eat Jesus' body and drink His blood?' or "How did Noah get all those animals on the ark?" We've talked about prayer and how it's like talking to your best friend. Each question is a small step in their faith.

When people ask why I go to all this trouble, I point to Timothy's mother Lois, and grandmother Eunice, who the Apostle Paul writes about in 2 Timothy 1:5. Though this is the only reference to these two women, we see what an important role they played in Timothy's faith walk. I particularly love how the Amplified Bible phrases this verse: "*I am calling up memories of your sincere and unqualified faith, the leaning of your entire personality on God in Christ in absolute trust and confidence in His power, wisdom, and goods, a faith that first lived permanently in the heart of your grandmother, Lois and in your mother, Eunice, and now, I am fully persuaded, dwells in you also.*"

Wow! Here were two women living out their faith and putting their complete trust in God! I bet they had Timothy at the temple's door every time it was open! What a wonderful example these two placed before Timothy every day!

That's the kind of example I want to be to my children and grandchildren every day of my life.

Application Question:

How are you helping your children/grandchildren grow in their faith?

Prayer:

Lord, take what I have and use it to Your glory. Give me a willing heart to give without question. In Jesus' name I pray. Amen.

Patty Smith Hall is a multi-published author, teacher and encourager to new writers just starting their journey. A founding member of ACFW (American Christian Fiction Writers), she served on the national board and as a Genesis contest coordinator and presided as president of her local chapter. As an acquisition editor for Winged Publications, she finds great joy in helping and encouraging others reach their publishing dreams. Married almost 40 years to Danny, she enjoys time spent with her family, friends, and in her relationship with Jesus Christ. You can connect with her at www.pattysmithhall.com.

Timothy's Instruction... for a Senior?

VERNET CLEMONS NETTLES

"...when I call to remembrance the genuine faith that is in you, which dwelt first in your grandmother Lois and your mother Eunice, and I am persuaded is in you also. Therefore I remind you to stir up the gift of God which is in you through the laying on of my hands."

2 TIMOTHY 1:5-6

In 2 Timothy 1:5, Paul mentions Lois, Timothy's grandmother, and his mother, Eunice. He speaks of their faith. Then he seems to remind Timothy that their faith also resided in him. Which leads me to wonder what faith have we left with our grandchildren and children?

Raising our children is one of the most precious and challenging Godly missions we have been assigned. We look at these cute little people and think, "Oh Lord, what am I going to do?" Sometimes we rely on how our parents raised us, hoping that our faded memories of fun and faux pas would guide us to raise "good children." Sometimes we pray in exasperation, "Lord, what am I going to do with this child??!!"

But over the years of raising my daughter, I have realized that we should truly rely on God from the moment we know that we are bringing a new life into this world. We teach our teens that God has a purpose for them. We should begin the conversation as soon as possible. I used to pray for my daughter's strength and personality—stating what I wanted God to place in her. I failed to realize that the parenting challenge is knowing God already has a plan and purpose for our little people. Our prayer should ask God to show us their developing talents so that we cultivate His gifts in them.

While raising our children, we tell them a lot of things. We spend time talking around the dinner table or before bedtime, encouraging them to dream, work harder, share their thoughts, be humble, be strong, be kind, and so many other life nuggets. We hope that these conversations encourage them and become their foundation. But, truthfully, sometimes we become discouraged because their lives often take different paths, and we wonder if they have heard anything we've said.

Our encouragement, however, comes from Paul as he tells Timothy to stir up the spiritual gifts given him by his grandmother and mother. Although we cannot always immediately see the results, our children do hear us and store our words. I may not remember each word from my parents, but my intuition kicks in, and I realize my success is because of something my parents said or did.

My grandfather caught fresh fish and gave it to his family and neighbors. He taught us to be giving. My grandmother waited for us to come home from elementary school. She taught us to be expectant. My maternal grandmother uniquely celebrated our birthdays. She taught us self-worth. My father owned two pharmacies. He taught us entrepreneurship and community. My mother was a homemaker, caregiver, and sales consultant. She taught us perseverance against the odds.

We may not always know which aspects we have poured into our children that will surface. But we must trust that our faith and walk with God becomes their example. Eunice and Lois were well-known for their faith. Although they are only mentioned a few times in scripture, each time they are mentioned, there is an expression of their faith. We are led to believe that they poured faith and examples into Timothy and their family.

What have we poured into our children and grandchildren? Are our lives examples of our faith walk with God? Are our words examples of prayers to our Father? Are our behaviors examples of treating each other with kindness and brotherly love?

We can be assured that God will bring to light all that we have poured into our children. We can be assured that the light of Christ we have shown will continue to shine within them.

With life's challenges, each of us—adults and children—can often become distracted and discouraged. But when our children heed Paul's words to stir up the gift, they will stir up all that has been poured into them and all that God has in store for them. Thank you, Lord. Amen.

Application Questions:

What examples did your parents and grandparents live out? If they were believers, do you recognize some of their faith as your own now? What do you hope to pass down to your children, or if you have none, to the younger members of your church or community?

Prayer:

Father God, thank you for our children, our legacy, our loves. Continue, Father, to pour into us your love, so that we can pour that love into our children. Remind us that you have already bestowed gifts and talents into these little people. Guide us to stir up their gifts so that they feel your

*joy in each step—so that they, too, can eventually stir up
their gifts with the love and life of Christ in their hearts.
In Jesus' name we pray and praise you in advance. Amen.*

Vernet Clemons Nettles, EdD is a parent, educator, author, speaker, and poet. Currently residing in Montgomery, Alabama, she has served in various capacities of church service. Now a retired educator, Dr. Nettles believes she has fulfilled her dream of working in education to serve youth and adults in multiple areas of the education arena and looks forward to all that God has in store in life's newest chapter. Dr. Nettles also shares daily original prayers that focus on spiritual growth and connecting with God on her website Another Day's Journey at www.vcndailypray.com. More information can be found at www.vernetcnettles.com.

Lois & Eunice (Timothy's Grandmother and Mother)

Lois and Eunice beamed at each other as they talked about the letters Paul had written to their grandson and son, Timothy. Paul had given Timothy a glowing review when it came to his steadfast faith. They basked in the joy of it all.

In this chapter we'll discuss who these two godly women are. You may have heard their names spoken together over the years as Timothy's grandmother and mother. But, like me, you might have had trouble telling them apart. So first, let me introduce Lois—Timothy's grandmother. Lois would probably be in her winter season like us.

Then there's Eunice, Timothy's mother. We'll discuss their faith and how it made such a deep impression on Timothy—and how we, as mothers and grandmothers, can influence our children and grandchildren.

We will discuss our ability to influence our children even when we've done everything we possibly could, and our children's lives don't turn out as we had dreamed. We will learn that it doesn't mean we are a failure, and everything we do to honor God will make a lasting impression on them even if we don't see the results now.

Let's look at what Edith Deen has to say about these two women and their influence on Timothy:

Timothy the son, Eunice the mother, and Lois the grandmother represents the strongest spiritual trio stemming from
the maternal line of any family group in the New Testament.
The sublime faith of the mother and grandmother seems to
have prepared the son for that greatest of all compliments,
which Paul later bestowed when he called him, "my dearly
beloved son" (2 Timothy 1:2).

Paul brought this out several times in I and II Timothy.
Only because of the early training that he had received from
his mother and grandmother could Timothy earn this fond
term from the childless and wifeless Paul. The latter loved
Timothy as if he were his own son and spoke of him always
with genuine pride (*All of the Women of the Bible*).

Timothy's story is told in 1 and 2 Timothy. Paul wrote to
Timothy often with wisdom and encouragement while Timothy
was overseeing a group of Christians.

**Read 1 Timothy 1:1-3 and write down the city where Paul
encouraged Timothy to stay and teach. What instructions did
Paul give Timothy concerning this congregation?**

*This letter is from Paul, an apostle of Christ Jesus, appointed by
the command of God our Savior and Christ Jesus, who gives us
hope. I am writing to Timothy, true son in the faith. May God
the Father and Christ Jesus our Lord give you grace, mercy,
and peace. When I left for Macedonia, I urged you to stay in
Ephesus and stop those whose teaching is contrary to the truth.
Don't let them waste their time in endless discussion of myths
and spiritual pedigrees. These things only lead to meaningless
speculations, which don't help people have a life of faith in God.*

1 Timothy 1:1-3 NLT

_____
_____
_____
_____
_____
_____
_____
_____

According to Acts 16:1 what was Timothy's heritage?

Paul went first to Derbe and then to Lystra, where there was a young disciple named Timothy. His mother was a Jewish believer, but his father was a Greek.

Acts 16:1 NLT

_____
_____
_____
_____
_____
_____

Timothy's father is not mentioned in his upbringing. This leads us to believe that possibly he had died and left Eunice to raise Timothy on her own. Grandma Lois stepped up and helped Eunice with this responsibility. Perhaps Eunice had to go out and glean in the fields to get enough food for them or find another occupation, and Lois watched Timothy during the day. During this time, I imagine Lois regaled Timothy with stories of old and by the time he was a teenager, he was well versed in Jewish history and their faith.

Write down several verses from 1 and 2 Timothy that highlight Lois and Eunice's influence on Timothy.

_____

_____

_____

_____

_____

_____

_____

_____

Eunice and Lois symbolize how mothers and grandmothers can positively influence their children to do great things. These women of the first century AD were raised as Jews and converted to Christianity during one of Apostle Paul's missionary trips to their home in Lystra. Despite a patriarchal system and male-dominated society, Timothy (a convert and companion of Paul) isn't identified by the name of his father, but instead by his mother, Eunice. Although Eunice and her mother, Lois, are referenced only briefly in the Bible, the context in which their names appear speaks volumes. The implication is that Eunice and Lois together lay the foundation for Timothy's faith (2 Timothy 2:5, *Women in the Bible for Dummies*).

We've spent a good bit of time on the best possible outcome of a mother and grandmother's influence on children and grandchildren. But no matter how hard we try to be an example to our children they ultimately have free will to choose. And they don't always choose the best route at the time.

I look back and think of my parents as examples in my life. Mother was sick and unable to go to church most of the time. But Dad would be there with me and my two brothers every time the doors were open. And I mean that literally—twice on Sundays and then on Wednesday nights without fail. This lasted until we were adults.

However, our life was anything but calm at home. As a result of Mother being so sick with Rheumatoid Arthritis and being in and out of the hospital, Dad carried a lot of responsibility. He had grown up in a rural part of Alabama and lost his mother when he was four. His dad remarried a girl younger than his oldest sister and started a new family. There were twelve siblings in Dad's family. When he was old enough, he moved in with his sister, and she helped raise him. They were poor, and Dad only went through the sixth grade before he had to quit and work on the farm. In other words, he had his own childhood baggage to carry around, as well as taking care of his wife and three rambunctious children.

The following excerpt is taken from my book, *Blooming in Broken Places.*

> From the outside, our family seemed normal, and just like everyone else's in our suburban neighborhood. We lived in a nice wood-framed house just outside the city limits. The house sat on a hill with a big field at the bottom where we'd play baseball and other sports with the neighborhood kids. I have memories of living there that are as sweet as the succulent red rose bushes that stood sentry between the side of the house and the woods. But life wasn't always rosy.
>
> Inside the little house on the hill, storms brewed frequently. Dad had a temper as big as he was. Even though

Mother was disabled there were times Dad hit her. I remember Mother taking us kids in the middle of the night to her friend's house and when she opened the door I blurted through tears, "Daddy hit Mother again." The image of us standing in that doorway still haunts me.

Eventually, as we children got older and were able to take on some of the responsibility, the physical abuse stopped, but the turmoil never did. We all carry scars from our childhood, and Dad was no different. He had scars of his own.

I knew Mother and Dad were trying their best to raise us in a Christian home. But it was not a peaceful existence. I've told you all this not to make my parents look like failures but to show even when brought up in "not so perfect" circumstances, the seeds they planted in my brothers and my life grew despite it not being a perfect environment.

Because of my upbringing, I, too, had baggage, and my children lived in an environment much like the one I grew up in. But the beauty of this story is to show that God can and will take our messes and use them as messages. I've been writing Christian books for twenty years now, as well as speaking all around the South. My last two nonfiction books centered around my life and those of twelve women from the Bible who were broken but God used them anyway. I know that my parents' examples ultimately led me on my path to serve God. Both of my brothers follow Jesus as well.

There are many examples of Godly men whose children went astray. In Samuel, we read about Eli, the priest at Shiloh, and his two sons.

Read 1 Samuel 2:22-25 and write down what Eli's two sons were doing to displease God.

Now Eli was very old, but he was aware of what his sons were doing to the people of Israel. He knew, for instance, that his sons were seducing the young women who assisted at the entrance of the Tabernacle. Eli said to them, "I have been hearing reports from all the people about the wicked things you are doing. Why do you keep sinning? You must stop my sons! The reports I hear among the Lord's people are not good. If someone sins against another person, God can mediate for the guilty party. But if someone sins against the Lord, who can intercede?" But Eli's sons wouldn't listen to their father, for the Lord was already planning to put them to death.

1 Samuel 2:22-25 NLT

_____

_____

_____

Can you find more examples of Godly parents whose children went astray? Write them below. Do you have a prodigal child or know someone who does?

_____

_____

_____

_____

_____

When I was reading the devotions for this chapter, there were a couple of statements made that hit home with me.

"Lois and Eunice's faithfulness speaks to us today, reminding us to unashamedly demonstrate our love for the Lord. When you have opportunities to share your faith (with or without words) with your children and grandchildren, know that you could be influencing generations to come!" (Deloris Liesner)

This is what Vernet Nettles had to say:

"Our encouragement, however, comes from Paul as he tells Timothy to stir up the gift that is in him from his mother and grandmother. Although we cannot see the results, our children do hear us and store our words. I may not remember each word from my parents, but my intuition kicks in and I realize that my success is because of something my parents said or did."

Write down any other insights that may have resonated with you in any of the devotions for this chapter.

_____

_____

_____

_____

_____

_____

_____

_____

I want to give one last example of parents who did everything right but had no idea of the route their "perfect" child would choose to take. It would forever change their lives, as well as the lives of others. When I started attending and speaking at writer's conferences, I began to meet many women of faith and prayer warriors for God. One such lady was Carol Kent.

I had gone to a conference in Cincinnati, Ohio where I had the pleasure of meeting so many women of faith who lived to share God's message with other women (and men). Carol walked to the podium with poise and confidence. She was beautiful in her professionally coordinated outfit. My first thought was, "Wow! This woman has it together. I wish I could be a speaker like her one day." Little did I know her testimony would shake me to the core.

I listened intently while Carol shared their story. Carol and Gene Kent lived in Michigan and raised one son, Jason. From childhood Jason was an exceptional child: smart, funny, charming, energetic, and ambitious. Carol recalled if they could have chosen the perfect child, it would have been Jason. He continued to thrive through high school, and when he graduated, he was admitted to the prestigious Annapolis Naval Academy, where he flourished. He was then stationed in Florida to continue his training.

There he met his future wife. She already had two beautiful girls, and the Kents welcomed them into their family with open arms. They became Carol and Gene's grandchildren. Once again, it looked like the perfect life. Until… one night, they received a call from the police in Florida. Their "perfect" son had been charged with shooting and killing his wife's first husband.

There had been allegations that the father had abused the girls, and the court was about to give him unsupervised visitation. Out of desperation and the feeling of helplessness, Jason decided to remedy the situation in the only way he could think of—and that was to murder their father. He received life in prison without parole.

You could hear a pen drop in the room as she recounted their story. Carol went on to tell how their lives changed overnight. But the most impressive thing about Carol's testimony is what happened after this horrible event. Carol and her family were determined to use this catastrophic situation and turn it into a ministry. They pulled up roots and moved to Florida, where they would be near Jason so they could visit him more often.

For almost thirty years they have been ministering for Jesus. Jason has been a huge influence on other inmates and has led many of them to Christ. He dedicated his life to living for Jesus and helping others live for him, too. Even if it was behind bars. Below is an excerpt from an online article.

> On October 24, 1999, Gene and Carol Kent's only child, Jason P. Kent, was arrested and charged with first-degree murder. An Annapolis Naval Academy graduate with an exemplary record, and a source of pride and joy to his parents, he was convicted and sentenced to life in prison with no possibility of parole.
>
> Carol Kent shares their story in her book, When I Lay My Isaac Down. "It's discovering that the cup of sorrow is also the cup of joy as we engage ourselves in understanding the upside-down nature of the cross. By sharing my story, I can give people the opportunity to find hope, and it's a helpful way for me to process my own grief." Her book, A New Kind of Normal, helps readers to make hope-filled choices in the middle of lives that are much more challenging than the dream they once had for their future.
>
> During this painful writing period, Carol and Gene prayerfully decided to establish a non-profit organization to positively impact inmates and their families. Carol shares, "While God would never condone what my son did, His mercy and grace abound. Our eyes are open to a whole new

world—the prison system. We now see needs we weren't aware of before, and doors are opening to help some of the neediest people in our society.

Ladies, our children and grandchildren are not always going to live up to the expectations we had dreamed of when they were children. We've seen, as with Eunice and Lois, the impact a mother's and grandmother's influence can have. But because God has granted us all free will, their paths may not coincide with what we had already envisioned for them.

But we've also seen examples of how a mother's and grandmother's influence can sow seeds that will grow into faithfulness in our children and grandchildren. Even if we don't see it happening right now. We may not see the fruit of our efforts before we pass through this life. But that doesn't mean it won't happen.

Write down several ways you can think of to influence your children and grandchildren in your winter season. Even if you are physically unable to do things for them.

_____

_____

_____

_____

_____

_____

So, keep that chin up and never give up hope that your children are watching and learning any time you strive to follow Jesus!

Chapter Five

LYDIA, JOANNA, & SUSANNA

Women, The Gospels, and Miracles

GAIL PALLOTTA

Go therefore and make disciples of all nations,
baptizing them in the name of the Father and
of the Son and of the Holy Spirit...
MATTHEW 28:19 NKJV

O nce, I interviewed a lady for an article about her family's unusual home, a large log cabin in the mountains. While there, I mentioned how much I admired the beautiful wooden cross in her front yard. She smiled and told me the following:

"The contractor, who lived on our property while building our cabin, was not a believer. Still, I talked with him about Jesus and His Gospel the entire time he worked on the house. When he finished, he brought us that wooden cross and quite a story to go with it. He had built the cross in two parts with notches to hold the pieces in place as a surprise gift for us. Because he wanted to see the cross all put together before he delivered it to us, no matter what he did, the cross wouldn't budge. He was forced to bring it, intact, to our property. Of course, I love the cross, but I also love what he told me. His experience building the cross, and especially his failure to disassemble it after numerous attempts, convinced him Jesus was calling, giving him a sign, he should surrender his heart, which he did."

This modern-day lady spread The Gospel just like Lydia, Joanna, and Susanna, who assisted Jesus by using their gifts for Him. Lydia, a dealer in purple cloth, owned her home, which was rare for women in Jesus' day. She was a believer but had never heard the Gospel until Paul preached in Phillipi. After listening to him, Lydia realized everything she had belonged to God. She then looked for ways to offer her assets to Him and began sharing her home to help those in need.

Joanna married a wealthy husband, Chuza, who served Herod. Ill from either an evil spirit or a disease, Joanna was healed by Jesus. Becoming a follower, she traveled with Him and used her funds to help pay for food and other needs of His ministry.

Susanna and Joanna accompanied Jesus to Galilee. Luke wrote that Jesus *"went throughout every city and village, preaching…and the twelve were with him, and certain women, who had been healed"* (Luke 8:1-3). Along with other women, Susanna and Joanna went to help anoint Jesus' body after His death. When they realized Jesus had risen, they were among the first to share the Good News.

Today women of all ages and walks of life have many opportunities to spread the Gospel, such as in organized places such as Sunday schools, Bible studies, or homeless shelters. The list goes on and on. But we should also keep our eyes open for one-on-one circumstances like the woman who witnessed to her contractor who wrestled with the cross.

Application Question:
Have you ever pondered Jesus' words from Matthew 28:19, "Go and make disciples of all nations" in respect to your gifts and talent, or has a small voice within ever compelled you to minister to a particular person or group?

Prayer:

Our Heavenly Father, thank you for your blessings and protection. May we look to you for guidance in all that we do, share your love witnessing to others and spread the Word about our salvation in Christ. We give thanks to you, the source of every good gift, and ask for forgiveness for our sins. In Jesus name we pray. Amen.

Gail Palotta, an award-winning author is a wife, Mom, swimmer, and bargain shopper who loves God, beach sunsets, and getting together with friends and family. A 2013 Grace Awards finalist, she's a Reader's Favorite 2017 Book Award winner and a TopShelf 2020 Book Awards Finalist. She's published six books, poems, short stories, and several hundred articles. Some of her articles appear in anthologies, while two are in museums. She enjoys connecting with readers. Visit her website at gailpallotta.com

Step Out in Faith

LORILYN ROBERTS

*But before all these things, they will lay their hands
on you and persecute you, delivering you up to the
synagogues and prisons. You will be brought before
kings and rulers for My name's sake. But it will turn
out for you as an occasion for testimony.*
LUKE 21:12-13 NKJV

When I get to heaven, one of the first people I want to meet is Corrie Ten Boom. Corrie lived a quiet life working in her father's watchmaker business until 1940 when the German Blitzkrieg invaded the Netherlands. During this time, the Ten Boom family hid Jews in their home to protect them from the Gestapo until a Dutch informant betrayed them on February 28, 1944. After saving over 800 lives, the Ten Boom family was hauled off to two concentration camps where Corrie's father and sister Betsy died. Corrie was released from Ravensbrück for reasons unknown on December 28, 1944.

Corrie's Christian roots ran deep, and despite persecution, she stood with the Jews during an unparalleled time in history when the Nazis murdered six million Jews. Would I have that same character of courage if faced with a similar crisis? Perhaps Corrie's selfless acts of love were inspired by women she read about in the Bible who also stood against a corrupt political establishment.

Joanna supported Jesus through her own financial means. She was the wife of Chuza, who managed the household of Herod Antipas, the ruler of Galilee. Imagine the tension in Joanna's heart as a follower of Jesus when her husband held such an esteemed position in an environment opposed to Judaism and Jesus in particular. Joanna's life must have been difficult as she faced persecution for being a Jesus follower. A woman of wealth, she needed nothing but only wanted Jesus, and she gave out of her own resources to support his ministry. However, Joanna's commitment went beyond supporting Jesus financially. She, along with Mary Magdalene and Mary, the mother of James, witnessed the empty tomb of Jesus.

Another woman of New Testament times, Susanna, exhibited extraordinary faith. Likely a woman of wealth, after being healed by Jesus, she accompanied the disciples throughout Jesus' ministry, tending to their needs. Lydia, a very wealthy businesswoman and considered the first European convert, helped the early church to not only survive but thrive during the beginnings of Christian persecution.

These three faithful women of God withstood the attacks of the Roman establishment, resistance from the Jews who had rejected Jesus, and perhaps were even criticized or ostracized by some members of their own household. Their faithfulness encouraged others to follow Jesus and formed the early church's foundation. Despite, humanly speaking, insurmountable odds, the fledgling church would someday reach the entire world for Jesus Christ.

Today, we live in uncertain times, not unlike the time of Jesus or World War II. Ominous clouds appear to be gathering. Our ability to follow Christ in this godless world may become so compromised, like Corrie Ten Boom, we may face death by persecution. At the very least, as we saw during Covid, we may be restricted in our movements, perhaps finding it difficult to worship corporately. We may be prevented from working at our chosen professions, relocate from our homes, or face separation from those we love. Will we have the strength of character to be a Joanna, a Susanna, a Lydia, or a Corrie Ten Boom? Or will we compromise with the world?

I recently helped an older woman get to the grocery store from her car. I steadied her gait and encouraged her as we walked, telling her Jesus told me she needed help. Perhaps the greatest thing we can do is be faithful in the small things. Then God will trust us in bigger works as we grow in obedience and wisdom.

> *But when they deliver you up, do not worry about how or what you should speak. For it will be given to you in that hour what you should speak.*
>
> *Matthew 10:19 NKJV*

Even if the world hates us, we can rest assured Jesus Christ will never leave or abandon us. He will be there in our time of greatest need. If all we have is Jesus, Jesus is all we need.

Application Question:

Will I permit the world to steal my joy, or will I be a woman of faith worthy of God's calling on my life?

Prayer:

Dear Jesus, please help me to follow You. Strengthen me when I am weak and fill me with Your love so I can do those things You've entrusted me to do. Amen.

Lorilyn Roberts is an award-winning author of fourteen books and broadcast captioner. You can find her on the web at www.LorilynRoberts.com. In her spare time, Lorilyn is an avid ham radio operator (call sign KO4LBS), and CW (Morse Code) enthusiast. Be sure and check out her latest book, *The Night Cometh: 20 Fantastical Short Stories* on heaven, hell, life, death, and eternity.

Embrace Each New Season

MICHELLE BENGTSON

*Likewise, teach the older women to be reverent in
the way they live, not to be slanderers or addicted to
much wine, but to teach what is good. Then they can
urge the younger women to love their husbands and
children, to be self-controlled and pure, to be busy at
home, to be kind, and to be subject to their husbands,
so that no one will malign the word of God.*

TITUS 2:3-5 NIV

Of all the things I prepared for in life, the empty nest wasn't among them. Yet, God showed me that life after their launch could be just as fulfilling or more so than when my children were at home.

I've lived believing that everything we do should be as unto the Lord and supporting the Lord's work. For the first thirty years of my marriage, I worked tirelessly to share the love of God through my private practice as a neuropsychologist working with my patients and in the home, raising my children to know the Lord. I loved what I did professionally, and I loved being a mother.

When my oldest son left home for college, I was unprepared for the grief I experienced from his absence. I visited him at least once a semester and called frequently just to hear his voice. I was thrilled about his emerging life as a young adult but was comforted by having another child at home.

Four years later, as my oldest graduated from college and began his professional career, I steeled my heart for what was coming just around the corner: my youngest son moving across the country to spread his wings and begin college. Aside from my faith, nothing was more important than my family, and I felt the loss, the grief, and the heartache when both were gone from the nest. The house seemed quieter (and the grocery bill was certainly lower). I wondered what significance my life held now that my children didn't need me as intensely or as often.

I think of what life must've been like for Mary when Jesus began his earthly mission. We know he had siblings, but we know very little about them. Did Mary grieve as I did? Did she suffer more than I did because she knew his ultimate destiny? Did she wonder about her purpose when Jesus left home?

We all go through different seasons in our lives, and God has a plan and a purpose for each season. As I pondered where to spend my efforts and focus in this new, somewhat quieter season, God reminded me of the admonishment in Titus 2 to older women.

In this new season, God has opened the door for me to encourage younger women: singles, mothers of littles, mothers of teens, and daughters caring for aging parents. We all need an encouraging word and a listening ear. And if we're open to his prompting, we don't have to look very far for someone younger to encourage and lift up—he will bring them to you! How will you let God use you today?

As we surrender to his will and his way in each new season, we can be confident that *he who began a good work in you will perfect it until the day of Jesus Christ* (Philippians 1:6 ASV).

Application Questions:

Have you experienced the empty nest syndrome? How will you let God use you today to fill that void?

Prayer:

Father, I come to You with bowed head and bended knee. There are times, since my children have left home, that I feel lost—not wanted or needed. Please show me ways in which I can fill the void that exists in my heart, spreading the message of Your love for us in all our seasons. In Jesus' name. Amen.

Dr. Michelle Bengtson is a board-certified clinical neuropsychologist and the author of the award-winning *Hope Prevails: Insights From a Doctor's Personal Journey Through Depression*, the award-winning *Hope Prevails Bible Study*, and Advanced Writers & Speakers Association Book of the Year, *Breaking Anxiety's Grip: How to Reclaim the Peace God Promises*. She is the author of the new release, *Today is Going to be a Good Day: 90 Promises from God to Start Your Day Off Right*, and the host of the top-rated podcast, Your Hope-Filled Perspective with Dr. Michelle Bengtson. Her ministry's goal is to restore hope, renew minds, and empower others to live in their God-given identity. www.DrMichelleBengtson.com.

A Grateful Heart

SHERYE S. GREEN

As you therefore have received Christ Jesus the Lord,
so walk in Him, …overflowing with gratitude.
COLOSSIANS 2:6-7 NKJV

What motivates you to support the Lord's work?

Are you moved to get involved because God has placed a particular idea in your heart that won't go away? Have you been invited by a close friend to volunteer with a specific ministry? Do you contribute financially because of your relationship with the missionary or ministry leader? Are you struggling with peer pressure to participate in an outreach program of your church? Are you driven to give financial resources because you want others to think well of you?

Three women named in the New Testament—Joanna, Susanna, and Lydia—had only one reason why they financially supported the Lord's work. Pure, unbridled gratitude. These ladies gave freely and sacrificially to support the work of the Lord, motivated only by the thankfulness that filled their hearts. Joanna and Susanna knew Jesus personally; Lydia came to know the Lord through the testimony of the first-century evangelist Paul. God used these women as supporters of Christian ministry to bless His church through their kindness, hospitality, and financial support.

Joanna and Susanna were among the women who traveled with Jesus and his disciples.

A woman of high position, Joanna's husband Chuza was the manager of the household of Herod the Tetrarch (Luke 8:3). Joanna was also one of the women who accompanied Jesus' mother to the cross and also helped prepare the Lord's body for burial (Luke 23:55, Luke 24:10). We know little about Susanna, except that she and Joanna knew one another as they were sisters of deliverance, having *"been healed of evil spirits and sicknesses"* by the Lord (Luke 8:2). So grateful for the miraculous transformation that Jesus had brought into their lives, Joanna and Susanna joined Jesus' entourage, along with other unnamed women, and financially supported Jesus' ministry *"out of their private means"* (Luke 8:3).

Lydia, like Joanna, was in the upper echelon of society, a woman of commerce originally from the Turkish city of Thyatira. Now living in the Greek city of Philippi, she sold expensive dyed fabrics of various purple hues. One Sabbath, while praying with a group of women along the bank of a river, Lydia encountered the apostle Paul and his partners in ministry, Silas and Timothy. Already *"a worshiper of God,"* Lydia's heart was ready to receive the message of salvation when preached by Paul. She became the first Christian convert in Europe. After Lydia and all in her household were baptized, she invited the missionaries to use her home as a base. Later, Paul and Silas returned to the safety of Lydia's home after their amazing release from jail (Acts 16:14-40).

All three women owed Jesus a debt of love as He had set each of them free—a freedom far more significant than deliverance from demons or lives of comfort and self-absorption. The Lord had given them the priceless gift of eternal life. An encounter with Jesus always demands a response. What will be your response to the life-changing work of the Lord in your life? Let your answer pour blessings that will further the work of His Kingdom.

Application Questions:

What are some creative ways in which you can support Kingdom work? How will your gratitude for what God has done in your life motivate you to encourage other believers?

Prayer:

Father God, thank you for all that you've given me over the years. Help me discover ways to take this gratitude for all you've done and turn it around to minister to others so they can see your love, too. In Jesus' name. Amen.

Sherye Green's writings reflect her journey of faith and explore the heart's inner landscape. An author, singer, and speaker, Sherye has long been intrigued by the power of words to shape people's lives. A former Miss Mississippi, Sherye has enjoyed two careers—in business and education.

The co-recipient of the 2021 Mississippi Author of the Year Award for Nonfiction, Sherye collaborated with World War II survivor and fellow recipient Mildred Schindler Janzen to write her memoir, *Surviving Hitler, Evading Stalin: One Woman's Remarkable Escape from Nazi Germany.* Sherye is also the author of an inspirational novel, *Abandon Not My Soul,* and a collection of devotional essays, *Tending the Garden of My Heart: Reflections on Cultivating a Life of Faith.*

Sherye and her husband make their home in Mississippi. They are the parents of a son and daughter who are both married. The Greens have five grandsons and one granddaughter. You can connect with Sherye at www.sheryesimmonsgreen.com.

Lydia, Joanna, & Susanna

T hree women. Three different backgrounds. Three Jesus followers.

What *did* these three women have in common? As we study this chapter, we'll discover the common thread in their lives. I've said many times over, Biblical women lived in different cultures than we do today—but their feelings, needs, and wants were just like ours.

The women from the Bible that I studied for *Bloom Where You Are* and *Bloom in Your Winter Season* have taught me so much about myself. I encourage you to get to know these Biblical women on a more intimate basis. One of my favorite books for studying this subject is, *All of the Women of the Bible,* by Edith Deen.

Lydia, Joanna, and Susanna were leaders and disciples of Jesus Christ during a time when women in their culture were not on even ground with men. All three women stepped out in faith to follow and support Jesus. Today, as women, we have the privilege to support Jesus in so many ways without persecution. We'll be discussing ways we can support Him during our winter season.

Let's dig into Lydia's life first. Who was she? Where did she come from, and why was she mentioned in the Bible? And most of all, what can we learn from her?

We first hear about Lydia in Acts 16.

After reading Acts 16:9-10, write down what happened to Paul when he was at the seaport of Troas.

That night Paul had a vision: A man from Macedonia in northern Greece was standing there, pleading with him, "Come over to Macedonia and help us!" So we decided to leave for Macedonia at once, having concluded that God was calling us to preach the Good News there.

Acts 16:9-10 NLT

_____

_____

_____

_____

_____

_____

According to Acts 16:11-12 where did Paul end up on his journey?

We boarded a boat at Troas and sailed straight across the island of Samothrace, and the next day we landed in Neapolis. From there we reached Philippi, a major city of that district of Macedonia and a Roman colony. We stayed there for several days.

Acts 16:11-12 NLT

_____

_____

_____

_____

Let's take a detour for a minute or two to discover a little about Paul's travels during his ministry. Paul's missionary trip to Macedonia plays an important part in Lydia's life.

Paul was on the second of three known missionary trips (some scholars say there were four), and it is estimated he traveled over 10,000 miles during these trips. Quite a few steps in all those miles.

> From Troas, Paul and his companions sailed across the Aegean Sea, making a pitstop on the island of Samothrace before landing in Neapolis and then traveling to Philippi. In Philippi, they spoke with women outside of the city gate. One of them was a wealthy cloth dealer named Lydia. After her household was baptized, she persuaded Paul's group to stay with her for a while. (Ryan Nelson, www.ryannelsonstravels.com)

Lydia was a seller of purple cloth. The expensive purple dye was made from thousands of tiny shellfish. Thyatira was well known for its dyeing and garment making and Lydia may have been an overseer's agent for a Thyatira manufacturer.

Purple was worn by government officials or royalty. Only the wealthy were able to buy the expensive material or allowed to wear it. We know Lydia was a wealthy woman and owned her own home, possibly two—one in Thyatira and Macedonia.

Let's read a little further to find out more about Lydia. After reading Acts 16:13 where did Paul find Lydia?

On the Sabbath we went a little way outside the city to a riverbank, where we thought people would be meeting for prayer, and we sat down to speak with some women who had gathered there.

Acts 16:13 NLT

_____

_____

According to Jewish law, there needed to be a certain number of men before they could have a synagogue in their city. We don't know for sure, but this could have been why the women were meeting at the riverbank. But Paul didn't seem to mind it was a group made up of only women.

I love the fact that he felt comfortable speaking to these women which included Lydia. From the very beginning, God has shown his love and respect for women. It is believed Lydia was a Gentile who worshiped God among other Jews. As we read further, it will become obvious God knew Lydia's heart and sent Paul in her path.

Read Acts 16:14-15 and record what happened next.

One of them was Lydia from Thyatira, a merchant of expensive purple cloth, who worshiped God. As she listened to us [Luke], the Lord opened her heart, and she accepted what Paul was saying. She and her household were baptized, and she asked us to be her guests. "If you agree that I am a true believer in the Lord," she said, "come stay at my home." And she urged us until we agreed.

Acts 16:14-15 NLT

_____
_____
_____
_____
_____
_____
_____
_____
_____

There are several takeaways from Lydia's story. She is an example for all Christian women today. I'll list seven characteristics of Lydia, and then you write why you think these would describe her.

Hospitality:

_____

_____

Generosity:

_____

_____

Faith:

_____

_____

Humility:

_____

_____

Open Mindedness:

_____

_____

Perseverance:

_____

_____

Good Leadership Qualities:

_____

_____

Lydia is believed to have been the first convert in Europe. We know she was a leader among business acquaintances and in the church established at Philippi. Lydia not only gave of her money, but she also gave of her time and graciousness. We might not be able to give a lot of money, but there are many other ways to give back to Christ what he has so freely given to us. Do we have an open heart like Lydia's to serve Jesus in our winter season?

Name four ways we, as seasoned women, can give of our time and of ourselves.

_____

_____

_____

_____

_____

_____

_____

_____

You might be thinking right at this moment that you are not able to leave your residence, so that means you can't be of service. This is not true. It is a lie from Satan—telling us we are no longer useful.

I have a friend whose ministry is to send cards to those who need encouragement or who are sick. She also has a list of people she sends texts to every morning (me included) to start their day off on a good note. I look forward to her morning texts.

I want to tell you about a writer friend of mine who lived in a nursing home for many years and was able to publish 75 books as well as over 300 articles. This is what Darlene Franklin had to say about writing from her room.

"Living in a nursing home might make some people feel like their world is small, but for me it has never felt bigger," explains Ms. Franklin. "I absolutely love writing and when I look back at the amount of books I've published, I can't quite believe it was me who wrote all of them! I've got no plans to slow down, and I have lots and lots of ideas still waiting to be put to paper. So, this year my goal is to publish my seventy-fifth book—and I'm pretty confident I can make it happen" (www.darlenefranklin.com).

Darlene died shortly after she wrote this in 2020, but not before her books sold over a million copies. A great accomplishment for anyone—but even more for someone living in a small room in a nursing home.

One service we can accomplish even from our bed is prayer. Praying for our families, loved ones, and those in need of prayer (which is all of us) is a wonderful and fruitful ministry.

List four things we can do in our winter season even if we are confined to our home, assisted living, or a nursing home. Think of ways you could be a leader like Lydia.

_____

_____

_____

_____

_____

This chapter is also about Joanna and Susanna. Usually, when you hear these names, they are spoken together. We can find Joanna and Susanna in Luke 8.

Summarize what Luke has to say about Joanna and Susanna in Luke 8:1-3.

> *Soon afterward Jesus began a tour of the nearby towns and villages, preaching and announcing the Good News about the Kingdom of God. He took his twelve disciples with him, along with some women who had been cured of evil spirits and diseases. Among them were Mary Magdalene, from whom he had cast out seven demons; Joanna, the wife of Chuza, Herod's business manager; Susanna; and many others who were contributing from their own resources to support Jesus and his disciples.*
>
> *Luke 8:1-3 NLT*

_____

_____

_____

_____

_____

_____

We know Susanna was a courageous woman. Her husband, Chuza, worked closely with Herod Antipas, who had John the Baptist beheaded. She was one brave woman. We also know Jesus healed her of evil spirits or a disease.

Susanna was grateful for Jesus' saving grace and risked being persecuted for following him. Since her husband worked in the courts, they were probably wealthy people. She not only gave of her time but gave financial support as well, like Lydia.

Just as Christ had willingly given them His gift of healing, they freely gave to Him. Christ has done many good things for us, including the ultimate healing from sin. Doesn't that make you want to continue to give back to Him for as long as you're able? I know it does me. And yes, there are times when I get tired and weary as Satan plays his recordings over and over in my mind—you are too old, you are useless, nobody needs you. Let's just go directly to the King and see what He has to say about that!

Read Psalms 92:12-15 and write in your own words what this passage means to you.

But the godly will flourish like palm trees and grow strong like the cedars of Lebanon. For they are transplanted to the Lord's own house. They flourish in the courts of our God. Even in old age they will still produce fruit; they will remain vital and green. They will declare, "The Lord is just! He is my rock! There is no evil in him!"

Psalms 92:12-15 NLT

_____

_____

_____

_____

_____

_____

_____

Can you find one or two more verses that talk about the benefits of getting older?

_____

_____

_____

_____

Below is a poem I wrote during my fall season, while waiting for my winter season with cautious anticipation. Now that I've arrived, I realized I had nothing to fear.

SEASONS

As she walks along the trail,
She is engulfed with brilliantly colored leaves.
Yellow, red, gold. Fall has arrived.
Winter is yet to come.

She stops to rest and sits upon a tree,
That has lost its youth.
Thoughts swirl through her mind,
Like the leaves falling around her.

She remembers the springtime of her youth,
The grass was green, there were buds on the trees.
Everything was new and full of wonderment,
Just waiting to be discovered.

The sun dances on the fallen leaves,
As do thoughts of summer in her memories.
The days were carefree and meant to be enjoyed.
Yes, she whispers, summer was good.

The seasons have come and gone so quickly.
Fall is already here, and winter is around the bend.
But winter can be a beautiful season.
She awaits her winter with anticipation!

Write a few lines that describe your seasons of life.

_____

_____

_____

_____

_____

_____

_____

_____

My hope is that after studying these women you will see your worth through Jesus' eyes. Not only are we worthy as women we are worthy as seasoned women!

Chapter Six

NAOMI & THE WIDOW WITH TWO COPPER COINS

Remain Courageous

CINDY POPE

Have I not commanded you? Be strong and courageous.
Do not be afraid; do not be discouraged, for the Lord
your God will be with you wherever you go.
JOSHUA 1:9 NIV

In a dream, my husband and I traveled to London. His sister picked us up at Heathrow Airport, took us to lunch then on a historical walking tour. Rain began falling, and the sidewalks became crowded. I kept getting shuffled back and forth between throngs of people and further and further behind my spouse and his sister until I caught a glimpse of them laughing and talking as they turned the corner and continued out of my sight. By the time I made my way to the corner, they were nowhere to be seen. Darkness settled in, and I had no idea where I was. I stood there on a cold, dark, crowded street corner of London, abandoned and completely lost.

Eight months later, my husband forwarded to me an email string that revealed his plans to bring his fiancé to England to meet his sister and their parents. What a way to learn of your impending divorce! Suddenly, I found myself emotionally raw, mentally in a dark place, and physically ill at the thought of being abandoned. The dream had become a living nightmare.

After our divorce, he suffered a stroke, which left him unable to stand or walk. He moved to England so his sister and nephew could take care of him. I felt alone, humiliated, helpless, vulnerable, and disgusted at the way he had disrespected and used me.

I laid my burdens at Jesus' feet while praying for comfort and guidance. One day I awoke from that period of darkness feeling the warmth and love of Christ in my heart. I *knew* God was with me, and it would be through Him that I gathered the strength and courage to forge ahead.

In the following months, I completed my Master of Arts degree, obtained a client for my writing business, volunteered for a local farming agency, wrote articles for magazines, as well as working on completing my novels.

I now understand and appreciate why God let me go through that dark and lonely time—He had planned to use me to spread His messages of remaining courageous, to not become discouraged, and to know that He is always with me.

Application Questions:

When major changes happen in your life, such as divorce, death of a loved one, loss of a job, major medical issues, family or financial crisis, would you have the courage to place yourself in God's hands? Other than praying for guidance and strength, how can God get us through those changes? How can we come to understand that He has a better plan for us?

Prayer:

Father, thank you for your blessings and thank you for my seasoned years. Father, sometimes I get discouraged when challenges overwhelm me. I know you can take my messes

and turn them into messages. Help me do this in my life.
In Jesus' name. Amen.

Cindy Pope is an award-winning author who has been writing since the 1990s. She has written profiles in lifestyle magazines, as well as contributed to literary journals. Cindy is currently working on her fiction pieces, which include a paranormal novel set in Woodstock, GA, and a historical medical drama set in Richmond, VA. Her educational background includes a Master of Arts Degree from Kennesaw State University, a Bachelor of Arts Degree from the University of Alabama at Birmingham, and an Associate of Arts Degree from Wallace State Community College. She lives with her three dogs, and one cat in Woodstock, Georgia. Cindy can be contacted at cindypope1958@yahoo.com.

Is It Possible To Have a Rich and Fulfilling Widow's Life?

MARLYS JOHNSON LAWRY

For this reason I remind you to fan into flame the gift of God,
which is in you through the laying on of my hands, for God gave
us a spirit not of fear but of power and love and self-control.
2 TIMOTHY 1:6-7 ESV

During the last few months of my late husband's life, I often awoke at 3:00am with a sumo wrestler standing over me, tying my stomach into impossible knots. Always at 3:00am.

It was the thing I feared most. Widowhood.

And yet, widowhood didn't play out as I thought it would. Yes, there were intense moments of loneliness. But there were also brave-making campaigns as I eventually challenged myself to do things my husband and I had always done together, like hiking all our favorite trails in the nearby Cascade Range.

There were gratitude journals I filled with lists of "1000 things I was grateful for." Then I'd write another thousand and then another. Instead of counting my losses, I learned to list all I was grateful for: children and grandchildren who wanted me in their lives, in-laws who included me as part of their family, the ability to hike tall mountain trails, baking cookies, girlfriends who meet me for Chai lattes and catch-up conversations, juicy watermelon, gorgeous fall color, knitting cozy things, fluffy white stuff falling from the skies, and … well, actually, the list is quite long.

I learned an outward focus. When my focus was on me, I felt my broken heart intensely. I began noticing those around me with their own trials and doing small things I could to help ease their burdens: visiting a young friend dying of breast cancer, training as a hospice volunteer, taking food to new widows, and generally loving on people. It was different from the lay ministry my husband and I shared as a team, but just as important in God's economy.

But mostly, I leaned into the strong arms of God and developed deeper faith and deeper dependency upon my loving Father. Before widowhood, I depended on God and my husband. And now there was no husband. But God proved Himself faithful over and over as Husband, Provider, Protector, Wise Counselor, and Trail Guide.

In a letter to his companion and missionary partner, the Apostle Paul reminded Timothy that God did not give us a spirit of fear. Brave-making choices, gratitude, an outward focus, growing deeper faith, and deeper dependency upon our Father in Heaven made my widowed life richer, more purposeful, and more joyful in the face of unimaginable loss.

Application Questions:

What could you do to practice setting aside a spirit of fear and picking up God's spirit of power, love, and self-control? Could you intentionally take on something that would make you a little braver and more audacious? Could you start counting all the ways your heavenly Father loves you? Could you look outward and help ease the burdens of other people?

Prayer:

Father God, please open my eyes. Open them to ways that I can help others see and experience your love. Let me be an example of how you can use us no matter what season of life we are in. Thank you for your precious son, Jesus. And it is in His name we pray. Amen.

Marlys Johnson Lawry is a member of Oregon Christian Writers (OCW) and Advanced Writers & Speakers Association (AWSA). She has been published in *Chicken Soup for the Soul*, Bella Grace magazine, and other national publications. Marlys is a contributing writer for several national and international web-based organizations and online magazines.

Marlys and her new husband Dan have a passion for helping people navigate the hard and holy moments, having negotiated a few themselves. You can connect with Marlys at www.MarlysJohnsonLawry.com.

The Widow's Mite

PATTY SMITH HALL

*Jesus sat down opposite the place where the offerings were put
and watched the crowd putting their money into the temple
treasury. Many rich people threw in large amounts. But a poor
widow came and put in two very small copper coins, worth
only a few cents. Calling his disciples to him, Jesus said, "Truly
I tell you, this poor widow has put more into the treasury than
all the others. They all gave out of their wealth; but she, out of
her poverty, put in everything—all she had to live on."*
MARK 12: 41-44 NIV

Guilt ripped through me as the offering plate made its way
toward me. Every cent of our paycheck was accounted for
between bad financial decisions and our oldest daughter's college
expenses. I understood I needed to be obedient in tithing. But how
could we give when nothing was left in the bank account?

I'm certain the woman with two copper coins understood how
I felt. A widow, she had very little to give. With no husband and no
sons to care for her, she had no way to provide the basics like food
and shelter, much less money to give to the temple.

Of course, there were those at the temple that day who had
plenty to spare. How they must have preened as they walked up

to the treasury and tossed large bags of coins into the offering! The other folks around would have taken notice, offering an approving nod or a self-satisfied smile.

But the widow woman is oblivious to all of this. She knows she can never repay God for all the goodness He's given her. She may only have two little coins, but they're His. She may go hungry, but she's confident God will provide. The woman humbly walks to the tithing box and places her two coins inside.

The widow has no idea Jesus is watching her from close by. How His heart must have broken as one after another gave as a show of wealth, not out of obedience to, or because of their love of God. Then this widow woman with nothing much gives all she has. What joy Jesus must have felt witnessing this humble gift of love for our Father! Though there is no mention of this woman again, I'm sure her offering blessed her many times over.

As for me, I pulled the last few dollars out of my wallet and put it in the offering plate, trusting God to provide.

Application Questions:

Has there ever been a time when you gave out of obedience to God when you didn't have it? How did God respond to your offering?

Prayer:

Lord, please watch over my grandchildren. Protect them and open their hearts to Your saving grace. Give them a mighty work in Your kingdom, Father. I know You love them even more than I do. In Jesus' name. Amen.

Patty Smith Hall is a multi-published author, teacher and encourager to new writers just starting their journey. A founding member of ACFW (American Christian Fiction Writers), she served on the board and as a Genesis contest coordinator and presided as president of her local chapter. As an acquisition editor of Winged Publications, she finds great joy in helping and encouraging others reach their publishing dreams. Married almost 40 years to Danny, she enjoys time spent with her family, friends, and in her relationship with Jesus Christ. You can contact her at www.pattysmithhall.com.

Peri-Widowhood and Living with "When?"

VALERIE DENNIS

*And the peace of God, which surpasses all comprehension,
will guard your hearts and minds in Christ Jesus.*
PHILIPPIANS 4:7 NASB

Most women in their winter season have experienced the phenomenon of perimenopause. It is described as a taste of menopause. For me, there is another experience far more difficult to experience than a hot flash or two. I call it peri-widowhood.

In March of 2022, my husband ended up in the hospital for a week, and because there was nothing more they could do, he was discharged into hospice care and sent home to wait.

A widow is defined as a woman whose husband has died. We all know women who have lost their husbands and have had to pick up the pieces and keep going. It seems incomprehensible for those of us who have not had to experience the gut-wrenching grief of losing a spouse. It feels like an impossible way to live. I wonder if these were some of the very same feelings Naomi experienced when she had to pick up the pieces and move back to her hometown to begin a new life.

As I write this, my husband is still with me. He can no longer work, cook a meal, take out the trash, fill up my car with gas, or any of the other things he did in his husband role. I do it all now. I wake up, and the first thing I do is check to see if he is still breathing. This is no way to start the day, but it is how I have started them for more days than I care to count. I am already experiencing that gut-wrenching grief mixed with confusion, guilt, and a little anger. I feel like I am practicing for a test I do not want to take.

Some days I am at peace with it all. And some days, I am lonely and angry and heartbroken. Other mornings I wake up and my husband is already out of bed. I breathe a sigh of relief. I pray that when it is time, God will allow my husband to die peacefully in his sleep. As he ambles up the hallway with his walker, I wonder if this is the last time he will do that.

My greatest and most enduring love has been the love of Jesus Christ. It has pulled me through some tough stuff. It has allowed me to be human in front of others. I had to realize I was not perfect, would never be perfect, and God can do anything and everything. No matter how tough the day gets, there is always God. Instead of wallowing in my grief, I give it up to God.

Then I pray. I am not afraid to tell God I feel alone. I am not afraid to tell God I do not know what to do. I am not afraid to tell God how confused I am. I ask for the help of the Holy Spirit to show me what to do every day because I feel lost and do not know what to do. I am learning to "let go and let God." To find peace in living with when.

Application Questions:

Have you experienced the gut-wrenching feeling of being alone? If so, what are some ways you can turn to others for support during this season?

Prayer:

Father God, I feel lost. There are times I feel so alone even when I am with other people. Help me to find ways to fill the void that has settled in. Teach me to turn to others and ask for help and remind me asking for help is not a sign of weakness but a sign of strength. In Jesus' name. Amen.

Valerie Dennis is a Navy veteran, cancer survivor, caregiver, and notary. She is an occasional writer who loves Jesus, pandas, tea, national parks, walking, and crafting. Valerie currently resides in Texas. You can contact Valerie through her Facebook page at www.facebook.com/valerie0826.

Naomi & The Widow With Two Copper Coins

Naomi stopped, turned, and looked at her daughter-in-law. "No! This is not right! You must go back to your family. You have no obligation to me now. You are still young and can marry again. Please, listen to me. I've been an old and selfish woman."

Read the book of Ruth to learn Naomi's story. Write a summary of what happened.

_____

_____

_____

_____

_____

_____

_____

Naomi and her husband Elimelech, the brother of a prince, lived a comfortable life in Bethlehem of Judah. But all was not well in Bethlehem during this time. It was a dark time for Israel—they had turned from God, and "…_all the people did whatever seemed right in their own eyes_" (Judges 21:25). Because of this God brought famine among the land. We aren't told exactly what prompted Elimelech to take his little family, leave Bethlehem and move to Moab, a pagan country. I'm assuming he thought he was making the best decision for their future.

Not long after they arrived in Moab, Elimelech died. Naomi's heart was broken. Elimelech had insisted she leave her family behind, and now she was alone in a foreign land. Did she become angry and cry out, "Why Elimelech? Why did you bring me to this God-forsaken land and then die and leave me all alone?" as she pounded her fist into the dirt?

Have you experienced this gut-wrenching feeling of abandonment? If so, write down what triggered these feelings—the death of a spouse, the death of a child, or maybe the death of a marriage.

_____

_____

_____

_____

_____

_____

_____

We're going to discuss widowhood in this final chapter of "Bloom in Your Winter Season." I haven't experienced widowhood in the sense that my husband died. But I did go through the grieving process when my husband filed for divorce.

I thought my life was over. I had just turned forty-five at the time, but I was so heartsick I believed I wouldn't live to see my fiftieth birthday. I've just celebrated my sixty-ninth birthday and have learned that we can reclaim our lives after catastrophic loss. Yes, it is a new normal, but this doesn't have to destroy our joy.

Naomi's story doesn't stop with the death of her husband. She also endured the loss of her two sons.

Read Ruth 1:3-5 and write down the names of her two sons and their wives.

> *Then Elimelech died, and Naomi was left with her two sons. The two sons married Moabite women. One married a woman named Orpah [that's Orpah—not Oprah], and the other a woman named Ruth. But about ten years later, both Mahlon and Kilion died. This left Naomi alone, without her two sons or her husband.*
>
> *Ruth 1:3-5 NLT*

_____

_____

_____

Naomi was alone now, except for her two daughters-in-law. The loss of the men in the family would have been emotionally devastating, as well as financial, as men were the prominent breadwinners during this time. At this point, she was heartbroken. At about the same time, she heard the famine in Bethlehem had ended. She wanted to go back home! She wanted—no, needed to be around her people. We would feel the same in our own grief.

Grieving is a solitary experience, but being surrounded by our friends and family can help ease the pain. When I wanted to research how the Jewish people grieved in Jesus' time, I went to my friend, Terri Gillespi, who is familiar with Jewish traditions.

"Common ways to show mourning in biblical times included weeping and crying loudly. Also, beating the breast, bowing the head, and fasting were often part of the process. Sometimes, mourners would sprinkle ashes, dust, or dirt on themselves and tear their clothing. Mourning was a time to remove jewelry and other ornamentation, walk barefoot, and possibly wear a goat-hair garment called sackcloth.

Typically, mourners would bring food to the bereaved—a very Jewish thing to do. The goal was to encourage the family to eat, even in their sorrow. Shiva (Hebrew term: seven) is the week-long mourning period in Judaism for first-degree relatives. The ritual is referred to as "sitting Shiva" in English. Sitting Shiva for someone is considered a "mitzvah," a good deed."

Terri went on to tell me when both her sister and sister-in-law died within months of each other, friends drove from Pennsylvania to Georgia to sit shiva. So, we can see why Naomi may have wanted to return home.

Though loneliness can be overwhelming, we are never alone. Let's look at some of God's promises.

Write down the verses below, then try to come up with two or three more verses promising God's comfort.

Psalm 147:3

_____

_____

_____

_____

John 16:33

_____

_____

_____

_____

Romans 8:28

_____

_____

_____

_____

But that is not the end of Naomi's story. Orpah and Ruth set out to follow Naomi to her homeland. But not long into the journey, Naomi entreated them to go back to their families. One of her daughters-in-law returned to her family with Naomi's blessing, and one followed her.

Read Ruth 1:14-15 & 18 and write down who went back to her family and who followed Naomi.

> *And again they wept together, and Orpah kissed her mother-in-law good-bye. But Ruth clung tightly to Naomi. "Look," Naomi said to her, "your sister-in-law has gone back to her people and to her gods. You should do the same." ... When Naomi saw that Ruth was determined to go with her, she said nothing more.*
>
> *Ruth 1:14-15, 18 NLT*

_____

_____

_____

_____

By the time Naomi and Ruth arrived in Bethlehem, she was in a deep depression. The entire town had turned out to welcome her, and the women asked, "Is it really Naomi?" I imagine her answer was unexpected and may have left the townswomen speechless.

If you are going through deep grief, there may be times when people stay away. Not to be hurtful, but they just don't know what to say to comfort those in gut-wrenching pain. If you've read my book "Blooming in Broken Places," you know that my daughter, Niki, was diagnosed with a brain tumor when she was four years old. When we brought Niki home from the hospital, she was left severely disabled. I was in that period of deep, deep mourning.

And some of my friends did stay away after we brought Niki home. I really believe they just didn't know how to deal with that kind of grief. I had one of those friends tell me not long ago, "Debbie, I'm sorry if I wasn't a very good friend. I didn't know what to say or do, and I felt bad because my children were healthy."

After reading Ruth 1:20-21A, write down what Naomi asked her friends to call her.

> *"Don't call me Naomi," she responded. "Instead, call me Mara, for the Almighty has made life very bitter for me. I went away full, but the Lord has brought me home empty...*
>
> *Ruth 1:20-21A NLT*

_____

_____

_____

_____

If we ended Naomi's story here, it wouldn't be very encouraging. But God didn't forget Naomi. As her story continues, Ruth meets Boaz, a distant relative of Naomi's. What evolves is a beautiful love story between Ruth and Boaz.

Read Ruth 4:13 & 16-17 then write down what happened after Ruth and Boaz married.

> *So Boaz took Ruth into his home, and she became his wife. When he slept with her, the Lord enabled her to become pregnant, and she gave birth to a son. Naomi took the baby and cuddled him to her breast. And she cared for him as if he were her own. The neighbor women said, "Now at last Naomi has a son again!" And they named him Obed. He became the father of Jesse and the grandfather of David.*
>
> *Ruth 4:13 &16-17 NLT*

_____

_____

_____

_____

_____

_____

Wow! What a storybook ending. But it didn't happen overnight, and it didn't happen before Naomi (and Ruth) experienced the deep valley of grief.

Let's take time to focus on life after the death of a spouse. You dare to ask, "Can there really be life after losing my spouse?" As I mentioned earlier, I haven't experienced this type of grief, but I have friends who have. I've seen them go from the pits of despair to leading a full life again. That's not to say grief and loneliness will never sneak up on them. It will, but there are ways to use that pain and turn it into something good.

Let me give you an example from 2 Corinthians 1:4: *He comforts us in all our troubles so that we can comfort others. When they are troubled, we will be able to give them the comfort God has given us.*

Can you give two or three other examples from the Bible of how the pain from losing a spouse can be turned around and used to help others?

_____

_____

_____

_____

_____

_____

We've spent a good deal of time on Naomi, but I want us to look at a brief account that packs a powerful punch.

Read Luke 21:1-4 and sum up what happened while Jesus was in the Temple.

> *While Jesus was in the Temple, he watched the rich people dropping their gifts into the collection box. Then a poor widow came by and dropped in two small coins. "I tell you the truth," Jesus said, "this poor widow has given more than all the rest of them. For they have given a tiny part of their surplus, but she, poor as she is, has given everything she has."*
>
> *Luke 21:1-4 NLT*

_____

_____

_____

_____

_____

_____

_____

This woman's name wasn't even given in the Bible, but I would say most people have heard of her. She is only known as "the widow with two copper coins (sometimes called the widow's mites)." But within these four short verses Jesus uses her as an example of giving.

Jesus wanted the people to know it is not the amount that you give, but the quality of your giving. Do we give with the right attitude, no matter how small the gift is, or do we give so that others will see us as we pass through the Temple?

When we go through the death of a spouse like this woman did, there will be changes in all areas of life. And one of those will be financial. During the time this widow gave her offering, there were no insurance companies, pensions, or Social Security. She was on her own. Jesus was very aware of this and knew she had sacrificially given more than all the other people coming to the Temple that day. Her gift did not go unnoticed, and Jesus lifted her up as an example of righteous giving.

As I read about this widow's giving, I had an epiphany. It is not just money that we can give. We can give of ourselves to help others. It's not how big our giving is—the answer is to give with an open heart.

Can you list several ways you can give of your time? Think of even the tiniest of deeds that would please God. For example: spending time with God, praying for someone or calling to check on a friend.

_____

_____

_____

_____

_____

_____

As you enter your winter season, there will be many changes and challenges in your lives. I've already experienced more than I care to list. I remember looking in the mirror and thinking, "Oh my goodness, how did my caboose get so big?" And it was pretty much downhill from there.

I think one of the hardest things to adjust to is the physical changes our bodies will go through in our winter season. I've experienced some of those changes, including a knee replacement. A couple of years ago, after I continually misheard words, to my embarrassment and my daughter's encouragement, I broke down and went to the audiologist. You guessed it. I came away with hearing aids. Now don't get me wrong, I'm thankful for the difference they have made in my life. But I told a friend of mine recently, "It's hard to feel sexy wearing hearing aids and glasses." We both enjoyed a good laugh at my expense.

But the good news is, even though we can't stop that winter season from coming, there are ways we can age gracefully. Are we going into our winter season kicking and screaming or are we going to continue to be mighty warriors for God?

One thing I've discovered is the road to healthy eating. I have a friend, Christine Trimpe, who is a Christian coach helping others on their path to better health. And I'm here to tell you that change isn't dependent on age. I know because I've experienced many of the good side effects from changing the way I eat. One thing Christine teaches that really resonated with me is, "Food equals fuel." Wow! I had never looked at food that way before. Not only did I change my diet, but I also changed how I fed myself spiritually. We are told in Jeremiah 15:16: *When I discovered your words, I devoured them. They are my joy and my heart's delight, for I bear your name, O Lord God of Heaven's Armies."*

Can you write down other verses that talk about the benefit of eating God's word?

_____

_____

_____

_____

_____

My friend, my prayer and hope for you is that by the time you've finished this study, you will see your worth in Jesus during your winter season. Remember, God can and will use you in your winter season. "He did not put an expiration date on our foreheads," as my friend and mentor, Babbie Mason, declared. Now, let's go and be God's winter warriors!

Acknowledgments

I've been blessed with so many supporters of my writing over the years. I can't thank all of you individually, but I want to thank you collectively. Especially, my readers, who keep me writing!

I want to thank and acknowledge the twenty-three women who contributed to Bloom in Your Winter Season, making this a unique work. They have helped make a dream of mine come true since I have been writing—to create a compilation with other authors. And what a blessing to have these extraordinary women write about their own journeys during their winter seasons.

And of course, my editor extraordinaire, Beverly Nault who has been with me from the beginning. Yes, she's a task master, but Bev has brought my writing alive for others to enjoy. Thank you, Bev. I also, want to take this time to thank my publisher, Brett Burner, who has literally taken my manuscripts and turned them into masterpieces.

Printed in the USA
CPSIA information can be obtained
at www.ICGtesting.com
LVHW022240310524
781759LV00007B/26

9 798869 255297